New Edition!

The official freebies for teachers

for

Teachers

**Something
for Nothing
or Next to
Nothing!**

From the Editors of *FREEBIES* Magazine

Written by Dianne J. Woo
Illustrated by Kerry Manwaring

LOWELL HOUSE JUVENILE

LOS ANGELES

NTC/Contemporary Publishing Group

Published by Lowell House
A division of NTC/Contemporary Publishing Group, Inc.
4255 West Touhy Avenue, Lincolnwood (Chicago), Illinois 60646-1975 U.S.A.

Managing Director and Publisher: Jack Artenstein
Director of Publishing Services: Rena Copperman
Editorial Director, Juvenile: Brenda Pope-Ostrow
Director of Juvenile Development: Amy Downing
Project Editor: Joanna Siebert
Typesetter: Treesha Runnells

Lowell House books can be purchased at special discounts
when ordered in bulk for premiums and special sales.
Contact Customer Service at
NTC/Contemporary Publishing Group, Inc.
4255 West Touhy Avenue
Lincolnwood (Chicago), IL 60646-1975
or call 1-800-323-4900.

Printed and bound in the United States of America

Library of Congress Catalog Card Number: 98-75619

ISBN: 0-7373-0064-7

10 9 8 7 6 5 4 3 2 1

Contents

Introduction 4

For the Classroom 6

For Kids 16

Crafts 40

Food & Drink 54

At Home 64

Health & Beauty 76

Pets & Animals 83

Books, Magazines & Newsletters 86

Travel 98

On the Internet 106

Sports 112

Odds & Ends 124

Index 127

Introduction

About This Book

Freebies for Teachers contains some great freebie offers that are sure to appeal to teachers and students alike, but you don't have to be a teacher to order from this book. Each offer has been described as accurately as possible to help you decide which offers are best for you.

Unlike offers in other "get things free" books, we have confirmed that each supplier wants you to have the offers listed in this book, and each supplier has agreed to have adequate stock on hand to honor all properly made requests. Many suppliers will make quantity discounts available. If you see something you like, write and ask about quantity discounts.

Some teachers have written and told us that they use the offers to set up a writing lesson. Students look through **Freebies for Teachers** and select an offer (be aware that some of the offers are not appropriate for children). The letter writing encourages good penmanship and spelling and teaches kids the proper way to write a business-type letter.

How to Use *Freebies for Teachers*

1. **Follow the directions.** Each offer specifies how to order the freebie. Some offers may ask for an LSASE (a long envelope with your name and complete mailing address with first-class postage affixed). Be sure to check the amount of postage requested; some offers may require two first-class stamps. Also, offers from Canada will require extra postage. Since postal rates can change, check with your local post office to determine the correct first-class postage to Canada. If a small postage-and-handling (P&H) fee is requested, include the proper amount (a check or money order is usually preferred). Some suppliers may wait for out-of-town

checks to clear before honoring requests. Do not send coins. Coins add weight, which requires extra postage, and can jam postal machinery.

2. **Print all information.** Not everyone's handwriting is easy to read. On your request, neatly print your name, address, the complete spelling of your city, and the correct abbreviation of your state. Be sure to include your return address on the outside of your mailing envelope. Be specific: indicate desired quantities and color preferences if the offer allows such choices.

3. **Allow time for your request to be processed and sent.** Some suppliers send their offers by first-class mail. Others use bulk-rate mail, which can take up to eight weeks. Suppliers get thousands of requests each year and may process them slowly or right away, depending on the time of year.

4. **What to do if you are unhappy with your freebie product.** If you are unhappy or have complaints about an offer, or if you have not received an offer within eight to ten weeks of your request, let ***FREEBIES*** know. Although the ***FREEBIES*** editors do not stock items or offer refunds, they can follow up on your complaints with any supplier. Suppliers that generate complaints will not be included in future editions. When writing a complaint, include the title of the book, the offer that you ordered, and the supplier's address. Send your complaints, comments, or suggestions to:

> ***FREEBIES for Teachers*** Book Editors
> 1135 Eugenia Place
> P.O. Box 5025
> Carpinteria, CA 93014-5025

5. **And there is more!** If you like the freebie offers in this book and want to see more free offers, then you should subscribe to ***FREEBIES Magazine***. Five times a year, ***FREEBIES*** sends you a great magazine with approximately 100 current freebie offers in each issue. Purchasers of ***Freebies for Teachers*** can get a special price on a one-year/five-issue subscription of only $4.95. (The regular subscription rate is $8.95—you'll save $4.00.)

For the Classroom

Pen Pal Exchange

Pen pals offer children the opportunity to make new friends and learn more about people and cultures in different parts of the world. Students in grades 4 through high school are invited to start a correspondence with an **overseas pen pal**. Send for a **FREE** application, directions, and helpful writing hints. All correspondence is in English. Founded in 1950, the World Pen Pals Organization is under the direction of professional teachers around the world.

Send: LSASE
Ask For: Pen Pal Info
Mail To: World Pen Pals
P.O. Box 337
Saugerties, NY 12477

Educational Comic Book

Learning about the U.S. government's Federal Reserve System isn't as plodding as it sounds, thanks to **"Too Much, Too Little."** This educational, 24-page **FREE comic book** presents a history of the U.S. monetary system and the events leading to the establishment of the Federal Reserve System. Geared toward high school students, this teaching aid provides a better understanding of how our free-market economy functions.

Send: Your name & address
Ask For: "Too Much, Too Little"
Mail To: Federal Reserve Bank of New York
Publications, Federal Reserve P.O. Station
New York, NY 10045-0001
Limit: One per teacher

FOR THE GIFTED AND TALENTED
Brochures

The National Association for Gifted Children (NAGC) is committed to excellence and equity for all students through differentiated educational opportunities, resources, and encouragement. The NAGC believes that modifying class curriculum based on students' individual achievements and interests is the best way to provide a quality educational experience. Two **FREE brochures** help teachers work with gifted students. **"Differentiating Curriculum"** lists books, videos, and journals on modifying instruction and curriculum, and **"How Can My School Better Serve Diverse Gifted Students?"** answers frequently asked questions on identifying and helping gifted minority students.

> **Send:** LSASE
> **Ask For:** NAGC brochures (please specify both titles above)
> **Mail To:** NAGC
> 1707 L St. NW, Ste. 550
> Washington, DC 20036

SUPER KID
Customized Certificate

Every child is special in his or her own way. Make a student's day by presenting him or her with a **Super Kid Certificate**. Each 8½" x 11" certificate is printed with purple foil on durable card stock and customized with the student's name and the message "This Officially Absolutely Positively Certifies That [name] Is a Super Kid." Suitable for framing, the certificate boosts self-esteem and a child's sense of self-worth. When placing your order, please provide the name of the student.

> **Send:** Your address and $2.00 P&H
> **Ask For:** Super Kid Certificate
> **Mail To:** Diamond
> P.O. Box 184
> George, IA 51237-0184

GETTING THE MESSAGE ACROSS
Rubber Stamps

Everyone appreciates the recognition that he or she has done a good job. Brighten students' spirits by stamping a special message on their schoolwork with a set of two **Good Student Stamps**. Each rubber stamp bears an encouraging expression: "You're a Star!" or "Way to Go!" Get these stamps and start spreadin' the news.

Send: $2.00 P&H
Ask For: Good Student Stamps
Mail To: Lightning Products
P.O. Box 16121
West Palm Beach, FL 33416

A DILL-LIGHTFUL LESSON
Pickle Lesson Plan

"A Marketing Dill-emma" is a **FREE comprehensive lesson plan** that follows the path of a pickle from cucumber patch to grocery store shelf and provides the basis for discussions of food production, distribution, and consumption. Aimed primarily at grades 3 and 4, the kit can be adapted for use at any elementary grade level. Included are activity worksheets and background materials, a packet of cucumber seeds, a recipe brochure for making Green-eyed Monster Burgers and other dill-electables, an approximately 36" inflatable pickle, and an illustrated poster outlining a pickle's journey from field to table.

Send: Your name & address on official school letterhead
Ask For: Pickle Lesson Plan
Mail To: Pickle Lesson Plan
P.O. Box 767 FB
Holmdel, NJ 07733
Limit: One per teacher

ROLLING IN DOUGH
Creative Dough Ideas

From making Indian fry bread to conducting experiments with yeast and sugar to sculpting dinosaurs and other creatures, you can perform a variety of hands-on classroom activities using simple frozen dough. **"Classroom Ideas from Rhodes Bake-N-Serv"** is a **FREE** illustrated **booklet** for use in grades K through 12.

Send: Your name & address

Ask For: "Classroom Ideas from Rhodes Bake-N-Serv"

Mail To: Rhodes Bake-N-Serv
Classroom Ideas
P.O. Box 25487
Salt Lake City, UT 84125

Limit: One per teacher

Web Site: www.rhodesbread.com

MCGRUFF AND READY
Identification Kit

Help students protect themselves and, as McGruff the Crime Dog says, "Take a bite out of crime" with the **McGruff Safe Kids Identification Kit**. Included is a child fingerprinting kit and a brochure on what to do in emergency situations. In addition, two full-color, attractively designed booklets teach Halloween safety and skateboarding, skating, and bicycle safety. Fun activities and nonthreatening language drive the point home in an engaging, upbeat manner.

Send: $1.50 P&H

Ask For: McGruff Safe Kids Kit

Mail To: McGruff Safe Kids
P.O. Box 931
Wayzata, MN 55391

TIME TO LEARN
Counting Frame with Clock

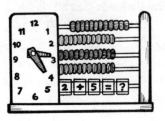

Teach students simple math and how to tell time with this **counting frame and clock**. This educational tool consists of four racks of movable colored beads, math wheels, and a clock with movable hands. You also receive a catalog filled with other offers for the classroom as well as for the home, including jewelry, arts and crafts supplies, and car accessories.

Send: $2.00 P&H
Ask For: Counting Frame with Clock
Mail To: Jaye Products
P.O. Box 10726
Naples, FL 34101-0726

STAMP OF APPROVAL
Teacher's Stamp and Sticker Set

A special **teacher's kit** is all you need to give classwork your stamp of approval. The kit includes a rubber mini-stamp with a cheerful picture or saying (supplier's choice), a set of teacher stickers, a flyer with creative stamping ideas, and a catalog of other stamp designs, from flowers and butterflies to whimsical expressions and holiday greetings. Start your own collection of mini-stamps. You also receive a coupon for $1.00 off any future order.

Send: $1.75 P&H for one set; $1.00 for each additional set
Ask For: Teacher's Stamp and Sticker Set
Mail To: Something for Everyone
P.O. Box 711
Woodland Hills, CA 91365

HISTORY LESSON
U.S. Constitution Booklet

Ever since the creation of the U.S. Constitution, more than a hundred countries worldwide have used it as a model for their own. Learn all about the greatest legal document ever written in **"The U.S. Constitution and Fascinating Facts About It."** Which Supreme Court justice is in the Football Hall of Fame? Why did America almost have a king instead of a president? Help students find out the answers to these questions and more in this 64-page **booklet**. It contains the entire text of the Constitution, the Bill of Rights, and the Declaration of Independence, and describes the men who wrote the Constitution, how it was created, and how the Supreme Court has interpreted it in the 200 years since its creation.

Send: $2.00 P&H
Ask For: Constitution Booklet
Mail To: Oak Hill Publishing Co.
P.O. Box 6473
Naperville, IL 60567

COMING FULL CIRCLE
Recycling Activity Sheets

With our increasing population and dwindling resources, recycling is a hotter topic than ever. A set of eight **FREE recycling activity sheets** from the Steel Recycling Institute teaches the importance of recycling steel and steel cans through fun word searches and a math activity. Students learn how to collect and recycle steel cans and how old cans are processed into new steel for use in cars, refrigerators, construction beams, and other products. The two-sided, 8½" x 11" sheets are reproducible.

Send: LSASE
Ask For: Recycling Activity Sheets
Mail To: Steel Recycling Institute
680 Anderson Drive
Pittsburgh, PA 15220
Limit: One set per request

KING OF BERRIES
Blueberry Poster

Cultivated or wild, blueberries are one of the country's most popular fruits. High in vitamins A and C and low in calories, they are used in jams, cornbread, pancakes, muffins, beverages, Danish and French pastries, and a variety of desserts. Brighten up your classroom with a colorful **FREE poster** that showcases this bounteous berry.

Send: Self-addressed, self-adhesive mailing label
Ask For: Blueberry Poster
Mail To: North American Blueberry Council
4995 Golden Foothill Pkwy., Ste. 2
El Dorado Hills, CA 95762
Web Site: www.blueberry.org

GIVE 'EM A GOOD RIBBON
Good Student Ribbons

The next time your students make a fine achievement, give them the recognition they deserve by handing out **Good Student Ribbons**. The ribbons come in sets of three. Choose from two labels: "Perfect Attendance" (gold lettering on blue background) or "Student of the Week" (gold lettering on red background). They're sure to put a smile on your students' faces.

Send: $2.00 P&H per set of three
Ask For: "Perfect Attendance" or "Student of the Week" (please specify choice)
Mail To: Lightning Products
P.O. Box 16121
West Palm Beach, FL 33416

A BITE OUT OF LEARNING
Educational Posters

Did you know that a poisonous snake's fangs are actually hollow teeth that are used like needles to inject venom? Or that the allosaurus could open its mouth so wide that its entire upper jaw acted as one sharp tooth to swallow huge chunks of meat whole? Two **FREE posters** feature full-color illustrations on one side and lesson plan material on the other side. The first poster contains fun facts about dinosaur teeth, and the second poster introduces basic information about animal teeth and human teeth.

Send: Your name & address

Ask For: "Power Bites" and "A Bit About Bites" Posters

Mail To: American Association of Orthodontics
Dept. CM
401 N. Lindbergh Blvd.
St. Louis, MO 63141-7816

HOLDING OUT FOR A HERO
Teaching Packet

Frederick Douglass, Thomas Jefferson, Clara Barton, and Cesar Chavez are just a few of the historical figures whose ideas and actions have influenced America's progress and its people. A 25-page **teaching packet, "America's Heroes and You,"** helps elementary and junior high school students identify certain qualities in these great individuals that they can then nurture in themselves. Each chapter summarizes the life of one of 11 famous Americans, accompanied by notable quotes, ideas for discussion, and suggested activities.

Send: $2.00 P&H

Ask For: "America's Heroes and You"

Mail To: America's Heroes Offer
P.O. Box 161167
San Diego, CA 92176

BY THE NUMBERS
Flash Cards

Flash cards are an effective and fun teaching tool. Get students on the path to learning with a set of four **flash card decks**. The decks cover addition, subtraction, multiplication, and division. Each box includes 36 cards plus instructions. You also receive a catalog filled with other offers, including household items, jewelry, pet accessories, books, and sports materials.

Send: $2.00 P&H
Ask For: Flash Cards
Mail To: Jaye Products
P.O. Box 10726
Naples, FL 34101-0726

PUTTING IT TOGETHER
Stapler Set

No desk—whether it's at school, home, or the office—is complete without a stapler. This handy **stapler set** comes with not only a compact stapler, but also a staple remover and a box of 500 staples. You also receive a catalog filled with other offers, including household items, jewelry, pet accessories, books, and sports materials.

Send: $2.00 P&H
Ask For: Stapler Set
Mail To: Jaye Products
P.O. Box 10726
Naples, FL 34101-0726

BE NICE TO EDUCATORS
Teachers' Resource

The National Institute for Consumer Education (NICE) is a consumer education resource and professional development center for K through 12 classroom teachers and community educators. NICE offers a variety of training programs, teaching guides, and resource listings of **educational materials,** including videos, software, textbooks, and curriculum guides. Write for a **FREE** listing of current offerings.

Send: Your name & address
Ask For: List of current materials
Mail To: National Institute for Consumer Education
207 Rackham Bldg.
College of Education
Eastern Michigan University
Ypsilanti, MI 48197

THE CIVIL WAR AT A GLANCE
Color Map

"The Civil War at a Glance" is an ideal supplement for your history curriculum. From Fort Sumter in 1861 to Appomattox Court House and beyond in 1865, this **full-color fold-out map** tracks the course of the war. The map is divided into the two principal theaters in which major military operations took place: the Eastern Theater, the area east of the Appalachians near the rival capitals of Washington and Richmond; and the Western Theater, between the western Appalachians and the Mississippi River.

Send: $1.00 P&H
Ask For: "The Civil War at a Glance" (#126E)
Mail To: S. James
CIC-8A
P.O. Box 100
Pueblo, CO 81002
Web Site: www.pueblo.gsa.gov

For Kids

Novelty Erasers

Eliminating written mistakes is a snap with a set of 12 **novelty erasers,** a nice change of pace from standard pink or white erasers. The erasers come in the fun shapes of fruits, flowers, and animals and are sweetly scented. You also receive a catalog filled with other offers, including household items, jewelry, pet accessories, books, and sports materials.

Send: $2.00 P&H
Ask For: Novelty Erasers
Mail To: Jaye Products
P.O. Box 10726
Naples, FL 34101-0726

Paper Doll Postcard

This **paper doll postcard** makes an ideal addition to any postcard collection. Printed on the 5" x 6" card is a reproduction of a Victorian-era paper doll. The little boy is depicted with a variety of outfits and accessories. The original paper doll was used as a promotional item for the Willimantic Thread Company.

Send: $1.00 P&H for one; $1.50 for three
Ask For: Willimantic Postcard
Mail To: Joan Nykorchuk
P.O. Box 47516
Phoenix, AZ 85068-7516

BOOKMARK BONANZA
Foil-Printed Bookmarks

Enhance the fun of reading with a set of **three bookmarks**. Each bookmark sports a different image printed in purple, red, or blue foil: a set of stacked books, a dinosaur scene with the expression "Reading Takes You Places!" and a cute skunk accompanied by the words "It Makes Good 'Scents' to Read!" Great to give as gifts to your bookworm friends, too.

Send: $1.00 P&H
Ask For: Bookmark Trio
Mail To: Diamond
P.O. Box 184
George, IA 51237-0184

NAME OF THE GAME
Personalized Bead Bracelet

Make a young friend feel extra-special with a personalized piece of jewelry. This **glass bead personalized bracelet** consists of a name in black lettering on white beads surrounded by an assortment of colored beads. Please send in the child's first name and specify wrist size in inches or approximate clothing size. These bracelets are great to give as gifts, too.

Send: $2.00 P&H
Ask For: Glass Bead Personalized Bracelet
Mail To: Bitos Beads
P.O. Box 41-925
Los Angeles, CA 90041

IT'S A TROLL WORLD
Children's Books

Introduce young readers to the enchanting world of trolls with a pair of imaginatively illustrated storybooks. You get two **Little Troll Tales** with each order, part of a series of six 5½" x 6" softcover books. Each 20-page book contains a whimsical story accompanied by bright full-color illustrations.

Send: $2.00 P&H for two
Ask For: Little Troll Tales
Mail To: Jaye Products
P.O. Box 61471
Naples, FL 33906-1471

MAKE YOUR MARK
Rubber Stamp Kit

Whether happy faces, dolphins, music, or sports is your thing, you can leave a good impression with this **rubber stamp kit**. Send in a list of at least six of your favorite animals and hobbies, and the supplier will select six stamp designs that come as close as possible to your choices. The stamps come with easy-to-follow instructions for mounting and stamping. Start your own collection today!

Send: $1.00 P&H
Ask For: Six Rubber Stamps
Mail To: Ramastamps-FR
7924 Soper Hill Rd.
Everett, WA 98205-1250

STUCK ON STICKERS
Sticker Grab Bag

Stickers make ideal collectibles because they come in many varieties and are great for trading and sharing. Let Georgia's Gifts help students start their own collection or build an existing one with a **sticker grab bag**. With this offer, you receive a minimum of 60 colorful stickers in an assortment of designs, including a sheet of Safety Sticker labels for kids. Your bag may feature dalmatians, funny faces, goofy animals, and uplifting sentiments such as "Have a Happy Day" and "Keep Smiling."

> **Send:** $2.00 P&H
> **Ask For:** Sticker Grab Bag
> **Mail To:** Georgia's Gifts
> 3850 Rio Rd., #75
> Carmel, CA 93923

THROUGH A CHILD'S EYES
Tapes for Children

Plug into a series of song and story tapes for toddlers and preschoolers that foster the imagination and teach positive lessons through irresistible melodies and memorable words. Brighten rainy days and shorten lengthy car rides with rhymes, music, stories, and classic folktales recorded by award-winning artists. A **sampler cassette** includes Sarah Pirtle's "Magical Earth" and Lisa Atkinson's "The One and Only Me." You also receive a coupon for $1 off your first order.

> **Send:** $3.00 P&H
> **Ask For:** "All About Animals" Sampler Cassette
> **Mail To:** A Gentle Wind
> P.O. Box 3103
> Albany, NY 12203

ADVENTURES IN READING
Animal Bookmarks

With reading, every book is an exciting and new adventure into another world. These **safari animal bookmarks** are the perfect way for students to save their place as they take their educational journey. Each bookmark, in the form of a particular animal, is made of durable plastic and measures about 4" long. You receive either two or three bookmarks. Designs include a giraffe, zebra, tiger, and elephant (supplier's choice).

Send: LSASE plus $1.75 P&H for two; $2.00 for three

Ask For: Safari Animal Bookmarks

Mail To: The Complete Collegiate
490 Rte. 46 East
Fairfield, NJ 07704

FOR THOSE LITTLE MISTAKES
Miniature Erasers

A set of 15 colorful **miniature erasers** adds pizzazz to classwork. The erasers come in various colors and shapes, including an ice-cream cone, a pair of scissors, a horse, a frog, a strawberry, a pig, and a peace sign. Kids will love these adorable erasers. Correcting mistakes has never been more fun!

Send: $2.00 P&H

Ask For: 15 assorted erasers

Mail To: Lightning Products
P.O. Box 16121
West Palm Beach, FL 33416

THE ART OF MAGIC
Magic Tips and Catalog

It's true that magicians prefer not to reveal their secrets in order to keep the "magic" in magic alive, but veteran children's entertainer Gandalf the Wizard-Clown is offering to introduce young magicians to the world of performing illusions. Gandalf has developed a list of **FREE "Tips for Learning the Art of Magic,"** which gives advice on selecting a stage name, choosing a costume, acquiring tricks, and more. You also get a catalog of 35 mind-blowing magic tricks for beginners and intermediates.

> **Send:** LSASE
> **Ask For:** Magic Tips & Catalog
> **Mail To:** Gandalf the Wizard-Clown
> P.O. Box 190
> Woodmere, NY 11598

DON'T MINCE WORDS
Mini Stickers

With these catchy **Super Word mini stickers,** you'll never be at a loss for words when it comes to praising your students' efforts and achievements. You get 200 stickers, printed in an assortment of bright colors, that feature such encouraging sentiments as "Great!" "Hot!" and "Special."

> **Send:** $1.00 P&H
> **Ask For:** Super Word Mini Stickers
> **Mail To:** The Very Best
> P.O. Box 2838, Dept. TR
> Long Beach, CA 90801

A TOPSY-TURVY WORLD
World Globe Yo-Yo

Now students can impress friends and family alike by "walking the dog" around the world. Send for a **World Globe Yo-Yo** and start experiencing the ups and downs of this fun pastime. It's great for a minor lesson in geography as well. Get one and start a trip around the world today.

> **Send:** LSASE plus $1.50 P&H
> **Ask For:** World Globe Yo-Yo
> **Mail To:** The Complete Collegiate
> 490 Rte. 46 East
> Fairfield, NJ 07704

GET LOONEY
Looney Tunes Stickers

Are your students stuck on Bugs, Daffy, Wile E. Coyote, Yosemite Sam, and all the rest of those wacky characters that populate the world of Looney Tunes™? Send for a set of **Looney Tunes prism stickers** and get them started on their own collection. You get a set of stickers filled with favorite characters (supplier's choice).

> **Send:** $1.00 P&H
> **Ask For:** Looney Tunes Prism Stickers
> **Mail To:** Alvin Peters Co.
> Dept. 98-33-FM, P.O. Box 2050
> Albany, NY 12220-0050

MATCH WITS
Strategy Game

Fans of games like Connect Four and Battleship will love this **4 in-a-Row Strategy Game**. The game consists of a board and colored discs and comes in a compact size ideal for travel. The object is to get four same-colored discs in a row while blocking your opponent's attempts.

Send: $2.00 P&H

Ask For: 4 in-a-Row Strategy Game

Mail To: Alvin Peters Co.
Dept. 98-18-FM, P.O. Box 2050
Albany, NY 12220-0050

A GLOWING GOOD TIME
Stickers

No need to be afraid of the dark anymore—not when these nifty **glow-in-the-dark stickers** are on hand. Ideal for use on ceilings, walls, doors, or any smooth surface, these plastic, self-adhesive stickers are easy to use and nontoxic and give off a bright glow. Select from glow-in-the-dark bugs, stars, or a 22-piece dinosaur skeleton ready for easy assembly.

Send: $2.00 P&H

Ask For: Glow-in-the-Dark Stickers (please specify bugs, stars, or dinosaur)

Mail To: Alvin Peters Co.
P.O. Box 2050
Albany, NY 12220-0050

MUPPET MANIA
Picture Puzzles

Join Kermit, Fozzie Bear, Miss Piggy, Gonzo, and the whole Muppet menagerie with Jim Henson's **Muppets**™ **Jumbled Picture Puzzles**. The set contains more than 200 peel-and-stick pieces. Match the numbered stickers with the numbers on each grid to create six pictures featuring the Muppet clan. The pieces are self-adhesive, so there's no mess involved.

Send: $2.00 P&H
Ask For: Muppets Jumbled Picture Puzzles
Mail To: Alvin Peters Co.
Dept. 98-01-FM, P.O. Box 2050
Albany, NY 12220-0050

CATTY CORNER
Mini Stickers

Cats make great companions—they give a lot of purr-fect love and affection. Students can start or add to their cache of kitty collectibles with a set of **200 Cute Kittens mini stickers**. Each sheet has a variety of fancy felines with funny or cute facial expressions in an assortment of colors.

Send: $1.00 P&H
Ask For: Cute Kittens Mini Stickers
Mail To: The Very Best
P.O. Box 2838, Dept. TR
Long Beach, CA 90801

Super Grow Sea Life

Here's a sizable opportunity: With just a little water, students can grow their own sea creature. Place **Super Grow Sea Life** in a container of clean water and it will expand 200 times in size. Remove it from the water and it will shrink back to its original size over time. Super Grow Sea Life can be used again and again. Students receive one of a variety of sea creatures (supplier's choice).

Send: $1.50 P&H

Ask For: Super Grow Sea Life

Mail To: Alvin Peters Co.
Dept. 98-07-FM, P.O. Box 2050
Albany, NY 12220-0050

Invisible Ink Game Books

Seeing is believing—and learning—with these **invisible ink game and quiz books**. The solutions are printed in invisible ink that is activated by a special pen included with the book. Students find out instantly if their answers are correct or incorrect. Choose between two titles: One book contains challenging games and questions on sea life, and the other book tests students' knowledge of dinosaurs.

Send: $2.00 P&H for one

Ask For: Invisible Ink Game Book (please specify Sea Life or Dinosaurs)

Mail To: Alvin Peters Co.
Dept. 98-29-FM (Sea Life)
or
Dept. 98-30-FM (Dinosaurs)
P.O. Box 2050
Albany, NY 12220-0050

A TRIP TO TINYTOWN
Shape Books

Take a journey through the wondrous world of Tinytown. Visit the Bookworm Library, the Busy Bee Bakery, and the fire beetles at the Firehouse. **Two die-cut shape books** lead the way, filled with stories and characters that will entertain all young readers. With this offer, you receive a pair of 16-page books (supplier's choice) that are part of an illustrated six-book series.

Send: $2.00 P&H for two books
Ask For: Tinytown
Mail To: Jaye Products, Inc.
P.O. Box 61471
Fort Myers, FL 33906-1471

TOP TURTLE
Pencil Toppers

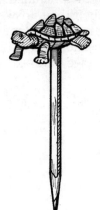

Turtle lovers will be happy to know that their pals on the half shell can now follow them wherever they go. A set of **three turtle pencil toppers** adds fun to both schoolwork and homework. Each turtle is different, with a colorful painted shell. Keep things slow and steady with these three realistic-looking reptiles.

Send: $2.00 P&H
Ask For: Three Turtle Pencil Toppers
Mail To: Lightning Products
P.O. Box 16121
West Palm Beach, FL 33416

ABRACADABRA, WHAT'S THE DEDUCTIBLE?

Magic Insurance Policy

So you're ready to tackle the spotlight as an amateur magician. But wait—do you have insurance? No master magician should be without it. Actually, Gandalf the Wizard-Clown's **Magic Insurance Policy** is not really a policy but a clever prop that is made to look like an official insurance document. It unfolds to reveal a 17" x 22" playing card. Included are directions on how to use the prop policy in your magic act.

> **Send:** $2.00 P&H
> **Ask For:** Magic Insurance
> **Mail To:** Gandalf the Wizard-Clown
> P.O. Box 190
> Woodmere, NY 11598

OVER THE RAINBOW

School Kit

This rainbow-themed **school supply kit** has everything students need to kick off a colorful year at school. The kit includes a zippered pencil case, pencil sharpener, pencil, ruler, and eraser. They're tools of the trade no successful student should be without.

> **Send:** $2.00 P&H
> **Ask For:** Rainbow School Kit
> **Mail To:** Jaye Products
> P.O. Box 10726
> Naples, FL 34101-0726

THE GNOMY-MOBILE
Friction-Powered Locomotive

Run your own rollicking races at home with the Gnomy® **friction-powered locomotive,** a replica of Lehmann's trademark "Stainz" locomotive. Available in yellow, green, or blue (supplier's choice), this adorable little locomotive measures 3" x 3". It also makes a great holiday ornament. With this offer, you also receive a color catalog featuring the entire line of Gnomy products.

Send:	$2.00 P&H
Ask For:	Gnomy
Mail To:	LGB of America, Inc.
	c/o Post Haste Mailing
	12260 Crosthwait Circle
	Poway, CA 92064

I BELIEVE I CAN FLY
Kiddie Wing Badges

Have you ever dreamed you could fly? Many kids do, and now they can have their very own wings. These **two Kiddie Wings** are gold-colored plastic badges that were originally distributed to children aboard the now-defunct Eastern Airlines and have become a cool collectible. Measuring 2½" long and sporting the Eastern Airlines logo, the wings are all you need to give flight to a student's imagination.

Send:	$1.50 P&H for two
Ask For:	Kiddie Wings
Mail To:	Joan Nykorchuk
	P.O. Box 47516
	Phoenix, AZ 85068-7516

MAKE A SPLASH
Bath Toys

Turn bath time into fun time with a bevy of colorful foam toys. Made of soft, durable EVA foam, these **Bath Fun Toys** keep young children entertained while they're getting clean. Each set contains six shapes in your choice of either animals or cars and trucks. The nontoxic, color-fast toys stick to walls or tile when wet, resulting in endless hours of imaginative fun and story making.

Send: $2.00 P&H
Ask For: Bath Fun Toys (please specify animals or vehicles)
Mail To: Neetstuf
P.O. Box 353
Dept. FR-149
Rio Grande, NJ 08242

HOP TO IT
Frog Mini Stickers

Get ready for some "ribbet-ing" fun with a set of **200 tropical frog mini stickers**. These ½" round stickers come in two sheets and feature an assortment of colorful frog heads in different designs and styles. They're great for decorating papers, school notebooks, and more. Send for them today and show your students a hopping good time!

Send: $1.00 P&H
Ask For: Tropical Frog Mini Stickers
Mail To: The Very Best
P.O. Box 2838, Dept. TR
Long Beach, CA 90801

MAGNETIC PERSONALITY
Funny Face Game

The next time young children are feeling bored or fidgety, introduce them to Hairy Harry. He's a **magnetic funny face game** that keeps youngsters occupied and out of your own hair. Harry is an illustrated face inside a plastic enclosure that is filled with metallic dust. The accompanying magnetic wand is used to move the dust around to create a head of hair, mustache, beard, eyebrows, even a funny hat for this stubbly pal.

Send: $2.00 P&H
Ask For: Hairy Harry
Mail To: Neetstuf
P.O. Box 353, Dept. FR-148
Rio Grande, NJ 08242

JUST YOUR LUCK
Good Luck Coin

Keep Lady Luck smiling upon you with this personalized **good luck coin**. What makes this fortune-bearing trinket special is that it can be personalized with someone's name or a particular saying or greeting of your choice. Send the name or sentiment (30 letters/spaces maximum) with your request.

Send: LSASE plus $1.00 P&H
Ask For: Good Luck Coin
Mail To: Great Tracers
Three N. Shoenbeck Rd., Dept. SS
Prospect Heights, IL 60070-1435

Bead Bracelet

Students can "bead" their friends to the punch by dressing up their wardrobe with this bright **bead bracelet**. This fun play jewelry is assembled by hand and features multicolored plastic beads on an elastic band. The bracelet comes in an assortment of attractive colors (supplier's choice).

Send: $1.00 P&H

Ask For: Bead Bracelet

Mail To: Bitos Beads
P.O. Box 41-925
Los Angeles, CA 90041

Personalized Stamp

Let people know that you came, you saw, you left your stamp of approval with a **personalized rubber stamp**. Send in your first name or any other wording and you receive a mounted rubber stamp with your name or wording in an attractive, catchy size and style. The cost is $1.00 for up to 10 letters/spaces, $2.00 for 11 to 20 letters/spaces. The limit is 20 spaces per stamp. Order more than 12 stamps and each stamp you order thereafter is half price.

Send: $1.00 P&H for 10 letters/spaces; $2.00 for 11–20 letters/spaces

Ask For: Rubber Stamp

Mail To: Lorraine Vetter
Ramastamps
7924 Soper Hill Rd., Dept. FR
Everett, WA 98205-1250

SHAPE UP
Magic Shapes Activity Book

With this **Magic Shapes activity book,** children learn basic shapes and have fun at the same time. No magic wand is necessary. All it takes is a pencil to make the magic happen. Simply rub or scribble the pencil over and around the shapes on each page, and a different surprise picture appears that incorporates the shapes. Find all 20 hidden pictures.

Send: $2.00 P&H
Ask For: Magic Shapes Activity Book
Mail To: Mr. Rainbows
P.O. Box 908, Dept. FR-160
Rio Grande, NJ 08242

FLUTTERBYE
Butterfly Mini Stickers

There's nothing like a bounty of beautiful butterflies to bring in the spring season. Send for a set of **200 butterfly mini stickers** to brighten up your students' notebooks, cards, homework, letters, and more. The butterflies, each measuring about ½", come in an assortment of colors and wing designs.

Send: $1.00 P&H
Ask For: Butterfly Mini Stickers
Mail To: The Very Best
P.O. Box 2838, Dept. TR
Long Beach, CA 90801

FELINE AND CANINE FUN
Dog and Cat Stickers

Whether your students are cat lovers or dog lovers or both, they'll howl with delight at these cool **cat and dog stickers**. Two sheets carry a total of 36 high-quality, real-life photographs of adorable feline and canine images. You get dogs, cats, puppies, and kittens of different breeds. The stickers are great for use on notebooks, in scrapbooks, or just to keep in a sticker collection.

Send: $2.00 P&H
Ask For: Cat and Dog Stickers
Mail To: Joan Nykorchuk
P.O. Box 47516
Phoenix, AZ 85068-7516

A JOB WELL DONE
Mini Stickers

Give students the praise and recognition they deserve by sending for a set of **200 awards 'n' trophies mini stickers**. Decorate their homework and projects with trophies, stars, and ribbons that will make them feel like winners. Each sheet contains ½" round stickers in a variety of attractive colors and charming designs.

Send: $1.00 P&H
Ask For: Awards 'n' Trophies Mini Stickers
Mail To: The Very Best
P.O. Box 2838, Dept. TR
Long Beach, CA 90801

THE BEAR NECESSITIES
Stencil Ruler

No student's set of school tools is complete without this creative **stencil ruler**. Use the durable plastic ruler to draw a variety of bear stencils. Students can create bear faces, paw prints, and a bear playing with a ball. The instrument is ideal for enhancing illustrations and other art projects.

Send: 75¢ P&H

Ask For: Stencil Ruler

Mail To: McVehil's Mercantile
Three Rasel Ave., Dept. FBSR
Washington, PA 15301-7120

IT'S YOUR TOON
Bookmarks

Let Buster Bunny, Babs Bunny, and the rest of the zany Tiny Toons™ characters help you become a reading Animaniac™. You get two officially licensed **Tiny Toons bookmarks** featuring a different Toon character in full color (supplier's choice). The character on each 7" bookmark is molded to appear three-dimensional.

Send: LSASE plus $1.35 P&H

Ask For: Tiny Toons Bookmarks

Mail To: The Complete Collegiate
490 Rte. 46 East
Fairfield, NJ 07704

Stickers
PETS ON PARADE

For students who love animals and stickers, these **pet prism stickers** make a great addition to any collection. The strip of stickers includes a rabbit, lizard, fish, parakeet, turtle, hamster, and cats and dogs. These shiny stickers are great for adding a little sparkle to notebooks, letters, greeting cards, and other items.

Send: 75¢ P&H
Ask For: Pet Stickers
Mail To: McVehil's Mercantile
Three Rasel Ave., Dept. FBPS
Washington, PA 15301-7120

Super Grow Dinosaur
GROW YOUR OWN DINOSAUR

In just 48 hours, students can have their very own dinosaur, right in their own home! Place **Super Grow Dinosaur** in a container of clean water and it will expand an incredible 600 percent. Remove it from the water and it will shrink back to its original size over time. Super Grow Dinosaur can be used over and over. Students get one of a variety of dinosaurs (supplier's choice).

Send: $1.50 P&H
Ask For: Super Grow Dinosaur
Mail To: Alvin Peters Co.
Dept. 98-08-FM, P.O. Box 2050
Albany, NY 12220-0050

CREEPY CRAWLY
Spiderweb Ornament

Come into my parlor . . . Fun for a scare or two at Halloween or anytime, this rubbery octagonal **web ornament** sports a fat black spider sitting right in the middle. Who will its next victim be? The web adheres to almost any surface via eight suction cups. Attach it to windows, sliding-glass doors, or anyplace your mischievous heart desires.

Send: $1.25 P&H for two

Ask For: Spiderweb with Spider

Mail To: McVehil's Mercantile
Three Rasel Ave., Dept. FBSW
Washington, PA 15301-7120

A GIFT FOR TEACHER
Teacher Pins

Give a little token of appreciation to your favorite teacher as thanks for his or her hard work and understanding. Choose from four charming **teacher pins** in the shapes of classroom objects: an apple, a pencil, a chalkboard, and an A+. The apple and pencil pins read "#1 Teacher," and the chalkboard pin boasts the sentiment "I Love Teaching."

Send: $2.00 P&H each

Ask For: Apple Pin, Pencil Pin, Chalkboard Pin, or A+ Pin (please specify choice)

Mail To: Lightning Products
P.O. Box 16121
West Palm Beach, FL 33416

THE WORLD OF BARBIE
Stickers

Even though she has changed over the years, Barbie™ remains a classic, creating fond memories for generation after generation of young women. Help students build those memories with a set of **Barbie stickers** to add to their Barbie collection. Each set of 10 stickers features Barbie in a different pose and wearing a different outfit with various accessories.

> **Send:** $1.75 P&H
> **Ask For:** Barbie Stickers
> **Mail To:** S & H Trading Co.
> 1187 Coast Village Rd., #208
> Montecito, CA 93108

STENCIL ME IN
Personalized Stencil

Help students make their mark in school. Students can enhance any art or writing project with their very own **personalized stencil**. Collect a variety of stencils and use them in drawings, scrapbooks, letters, greeting cards, collages, and more. Up to 10 letters and spaces can be used; just send the wording with your request.

> **Send:** LSASE plus $1.00 P&H
> **Ask For:** Personalized Stencil
> **Mail To:** Great Tracers
> Three N. Shoenbeck Rd., Dept. SS
> Prospect Heights, IL 60070-1435

LIKE A SECOND SKIN
Temporary Tattoos

Now you can enjoy the "art" of tattooing without having to get a permanent one! Start your body art with **temporary tattoos** in an assortment of fun, colorful, charming designs featuring dogs, cats, and butterflies. You receive six tattoos, each measuring 1½" x 2", that are easily applied and removed with water.

Send: $1.75 P&H

Ask For: Temp Tattoos

Mail To: S & H Trading Co.
1187 Coast Village Rd., #208
Montecito, CA 93108

A BIG HAND FOR A SMALL DECK
Mini Playing Cards

Here are two ways to "mini-mize" your boredom. Size up the **world's smallest deck of cards,** a novel addition to any miniature collection. The cards are large enough to use in a game. Or, go on a "small" safari with a deck of **mini animal playing cards,** colorfully illustrated with all your favorite animals—lions, zebras, elephants, and so forth. Either way, you'll be playing with a full, if not so large, deck.

Send: $1.00 P&H for World's Smallest Deck; $2.00 for Animal Cards

Ask For: World's Smallest Deck of Cards or Mini Animal Playing Cards (please specify choice)

Mail To: Alvin Peters Co.
Dept. 98-19-FM (World's Smallest Deck)
or
Dept. 98-21-FM (Animal Cards)
P.O. Box 2050
Albany, NY 12220-0050

THE WRITE STUFF
Pencils

When it comes to doing homework and taking tests, nothing succeeds like studying hard. But for that extra bit of luck, you can't go wrong with a **good luck pencil**. With this offer, students receive two pencils in different colors. On each writing instrument, the words "Good Luck Pencil" are printed in gold foil.

Send: LSASE plus $1.00 P&H
Ask For: Good Luck Pencils
Mail To: Great Tracers
Three N. Shoenbeck Rd., Dept. SS
Prospect Heights, IL 60070-1435

HOW MUCH ARE THOSE DOGGIES?
Mini Stickers

Dog lovers unite! Students will be in puppy heaven with a set of **200 Dandy Doggies Mini Stickers**. Each sheet of 100 stickers contains a variety of ½" round doggie heads in a variety of colors, hats, and facial expressions. Great for sticking on folders, letters, books, and more. Send for them today. Your students will be doggone happy you did.

Send: $1.00 P&H
Ask For: Dandy Doggies Mini Stickers
Mail To: The Very Best
P.O. Box 2838, Dept. TR
Long Beach, CA 90801

Crafts

Mini Teddy Bears

Teddy bears have been a beloved toy of young and old alike for generations. Now students can make a **stuffed mini teddy bear** to add to their collection. The **kit** contains two precut bear-shaped sections and sewing instructions for creating an adorable teddy. Adding snap-lock or sew-on eyes and an embroidery-floss nose is optional. You also receive a coupon for a free additional teddy.

Send: $2.00 P&H
Ask For: Precut Mini Teddy Bear
Mail To: Taylor's Cutaways & Stuff
2802 E. Washington St.
Urbana, IL 61802-4660
Web Site: home.sprynet.com/sprynet/tcutaway

Instructional Video

Encourage students to save money and jazz up their wardrobe at the same time by teaching them the creative skill of **sewing**. An instructional **video** from the Sewing Fashion Council teaches the ABCs of sewing and provides easy-to-follow instructions on how to make an elastic-waist skirt. Once students get the hang of this fun craft, they can create clothes and other household items for themselves, their families, their dolls—even their pets!

Send: $2.00 P&H
Ask For: "It's Sew Easy" Video
Mail To: Sewing Fashion Council
P.O. Box 650
New York, NY 10159

HARE IT IS
Stuffed Bunny Instructions

Equipped with a flour sack towel, rubber bands, safety pins, ribbon, and a few other household items, students can make their own **Fold-A-Bunnies**. The illustrated **instruction sheet** provides step-by-step guidance in creating an adorable boy and girl bunny filled with polyester stuffing. Suggestions for decorating the bunnies—such as dyeing the flour sack towel and placing small ribbon roses at the neck and ears—are also included.

Send: $2.00 P&H
Ask For: Fold-A-Bunnies
Mail To: Creative Corner
P.O. Box 1361
Apple Valley, CA 92307

STICK TO IT
Nontoxic Glue

Enhance arts and crafts activities and other hobbies with **Kids Choice Glue**. This safe-to-use glue provides instant holding power without the mess and frustration of runny glues, the heat from a glue gun, or the toxicity of solvent-based glues. It works well on paper, wood, felt, leather, cork, fabric, and more. Send for **four trial pillow packs,** each containing ¼ ounce of glue.

Send: $2.00 P&H
Ask For: Kids Choice Glue
Mail To: Signature Marketing
P.O. Box 427
Wyckoff, NJ 07481

HEARTS AFLOWER
Sachet Heart Kit

Hearts have long been symbols of love, romance, and friendship. Stuffed with potpourri, scented cotton balls, or fiberfill, these beautiful sachet hearts make pleasant additions to dresser drawers, closets, packages, and Christmas or holiday trees. This **Sachet Heart Kit** includes simple instructions, two pairs of 4" precut hearts, plenty of ribbon for hanging, and a coupon for free additional hearts.

Send: $1.50 P&H
Ask For: Precut Sachet Heart Kit
Mail To: Taylor's Cutaways & Stuff
2802 E. Washington St.
Urbana, IL 61802-4660
Web Site: home.sprynet.com/sprynet/tcutaway

A BOW TO PICK
Bow Maker

With the Little Bow Chic **bow maker,** it's a cinch to fashion beautiful, elegant bows to decorate gift boxes and crafts. The bows can be made from a variety of ribbons (including silk and taffeta) or fabrics (such as moiré and chintz). No sewing is necessary. Each kit contains two metal units and instructions for crafting 3" to 8" bows in four designs. Select either a ribbon bow maker or a fabric bow maker.

Send: $2.00 P&H
Ask For: Little Bow Chic (please specify ribbon or fabric)
Mail To: Signature Marketing
P.O. Box 427
Wyckoff, NJ 07481

HEAVENLY CREATURE
Angel Ornament Pattern

Angels have come down to Earth! This **angel ornament pattern** tells you how to make an adorable 3" tall cherub for your classroom's Christmas tree, wreath, or other holiday project. Included are a list of materials and step-by-step illustrated instructions for crafting your heavenly messenger. Have students create several to populate their own "city of angels"!

> **Send:** $2.00 P&H
> **Ask For:** Angel Pattern
> **Mail To:** Blue Fairy Crafts
> P.O. Box 295
> Gatesville, TX 76528

DREAM WEAVER
Dream Catcher Kit

According to Native American tradition, the night air is filled with floating dreams. When you hang a dream catcher at the head of your bed, it will catch and hold the bad dreams until they are destroyed by the first rays of the rising sun. In the meantime, the good dreams slide down the feathers to rest on your head. This **dream catcher kit** contains jute, beads, floral tape, concho, and feathers to make a 7" dream catcher. All you supply is a wire coat hanger.

> **Send:** $2.25 P&H
> **Ask For:** Dream Catcher Kit
> **Mail To:** Creative Corner
> P.O. Box 1361
> Apple Valley, CA 92307

A FRIEND IN BEAD
Gecko Critter Kit

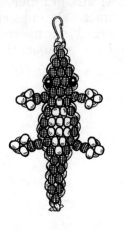

Geckos are small, harmless lizards that feed on mosquitoes and other insects. Live geckos may not be exactly welcome in your school, but here's the next best thing: The **Beady™ Critter Kit** makes two charming geckos that sport a colorful mosaic pattern. The kit includes more than 100 beads and two lanyard hooks for displaying these critter creations.

Send: $1.00 P&H

Ask For: Beady™ Critter Kit—Gecko

Mail To: Enterprise Art
Dept. #126
P.O. Box 2918
Largo, FL 33779

Web Site: www.enterpriseart.com

GET HOOKED
Crochet Crafts

Crocheting is a relaxing activity that is easy to learn and produces beautiful results, from handy pot holders to colorful afghans. Send for three **recipe cards** that provide simple directions on how to make a football, a graduation cap, and a snowflake, all of which are perfect projects for a beginning arts and crafts class. Lists of materials and suggestions for use are also included.

Send: Two loose first-class stamps

Ask For: Crochet Recipe Cards

Mail To: Crocheting Forever
20021 Fox St.
Cassopolis, MI 49031-9472

MOM AND ME
Project Sheets

The next time your class works on art activities, encourage students to bring their moms in on the fun at home with a series of **"Mom and Me" project sheets**. The illustrated sheets give instructions for five different projects using paints, stencils, dyes, and other materials. Mom and kids can make cowboy stencils, washcloth roses, decorative door hangers, autograph pillowcases, and colorful lunch bags.

Send: LSASE
Ask For: Mom and Me Project Sheets
Mail To: Delta Technical Coatings
Dept. FBTM
2550 Pellissier Place
Whittier, CA 90601-1505
Limit: One per request

A TISKET, A TASKET
Basket Patterns

Here's a great earth-conscious activity for students. Use brown paper grocery bags and fabric strips cut from new or old clothing to make practical, decorative **earth baskets**. Detailed **instructions** show how to craft a basket made of paper bags and fabric, and a basket made of paper bags and old blue jeans. No sewing is necessary. These handy baskets are ideal for collecting summer fruits, carrying picnic items, and storing magazines.

Send: $2.00 P&H
Ask For: Earth Basket Patterns
Mail To: Creative Corner
P.O. Box 1361
Apple Valley, CA 92307

A COLLECTION OF CRAFTS
Craft Recipes

Turn your kitchen into an artist's studio with five different **craft recipes** that can be made with items found around the house or purchased at a grocery store. An easy-to-follow instruction sheet tells you how to make ornament or jewelry play clay, finger paint, play dough, nontoxic children's paste, and crayon fabric paint using such everyday items as cornstarch, baking soda, flour, and food coloring.

> **Send:** LSASE
> **Ask For:** Craft Recipes
> **Mail To:** Taylor's Cutaways & Stuff
> 2802 E. Washington St.
> Urbana, IL 61802-4660
> **Web Site:** home.sprynet.com/sprynet/tcutaway

MAKE YOUR OWN INDIAN DOLLS
Doll-Making Pattern

Students can add to or start a Southwest collection by making a simple **Indian Brave Hanky Doll** and an **Indian Maiden Hanky Doll**. No sewing is required; simply begin with a white cotton handkerchief and incorporate beads, twine or jute, yarn, a rubber band, a feather, glue, and other materials as indicated on the **instruction sheet**. With a little folding, cutting, tying, and gluing, you'll create this handsome pair in no time.

> **Send:** $2.00 P&H
> **Ask For:** No-Sew Indian Brave & Maiden Pattern
> **Mail To:** Creative Corner
> P.O. Box 1361
> Apple Valley, CA 92307

BABY CAKE
Gift Idea

Who would have thought that a great baby shower gift could be made out of diapers, bottles, socks, and other baby items? Learn how to make this unusual **Baby Cake**. This fun and different project involves rolling up a baby bottle inside several diapers to form a round "cake." Wrap a receiving blanket around the cake, and turn up the cuffs of baby socks to make rosebuds. Then add lotion bottles, flower clusters, a baby spoon . . . It's all in the step-by-step instructions.

Send: LSASE
Ask For: Baby Cake
Mail To: Taylor's Cutaways & Stuff
2802 E. Washington St.
Urbana, IL 61802-4660
Web Site: home.sprynet.com/sprynet/tcutaway

FOAM AND FUNCTION
Foam Packet

These colorful pieces of **soft foam** can be incorporated into any classroom arts and crafts project. Nontoxic and waterproof, these materials are ideal for making cutouts and three-dimensional projects and for decorating hats, place mats, picture frames, and more. The foam sticks to any smooth surface when wet and may be glued to any object. Each **packet** contains 75 pieces.

Send: $2.00 P&H
Ask For: Fun Foam
Mail To: Neetstuf
P.O. Box 353, Dept. FR-159
Rio Grande, NJ 08242

THE SALT ALSO RISES
Salt Sculpture Brochure

Crafts and household projects should always be taken with a grain of salt—thousands of grains, actually! Table salt has more uses than just as a food flavoring, as you'll learn in **two brochures** from Morton Salt. One brochure has instructions for making **dough sculptures**—a gingerbread man, bell, star, or Christmas tree ornament—out of salt, flour, and water. Household hints are the focus of the second brochure, which describes how to use salt to get out stains, make panty hose run-resistant, and remove rust and odors.

Send: LSASE
Ask For: "Dough It Yourself" and "Household Hints"
Mail To: Morton Salt
Dept. FR
100 N. Riverside Place
Chicago, IL 60606

IT'S SEW FUN
Children's Brochure

"Sew Creative," an educational **brochure** from the Home Sewing Association, emphasizes that learning to sew helps kids become more creative thinkers. In a study, girls and boys ages 8 to 12 who sewed a simple project showed elevated creativity afterward. Such children also exhibit heightened self-esteem, problem-solving skills, and perseverance. The brochure describes the study and its results, outlines other benefits of sewing, and lists ideas for first projects.

Send: LSASE
Ask For: "Sew Creative"
Mail To: Home Sewing Association
1350 Broadway, Ste. 1601
New York, NY 10018

SKY ONE ON
Kite-Making Plans

With **five kite plans** from the American Kitefliers Association, the sky's the limit on the fun your students can have. The plans, which range from simple to more challenging, guide you in making a sled kite, a delta kite, a Vietnamese children's kite, a Japanese children's kite, and a box kite. Step-by-step, illustrated instructions and materials lists are included.

Send: LSASE

Ask For: Kite Patterns

Mail To: A.K.A.
352 Hungerford Dr.
Rockville, MD 20850-4117

PLASTIC POSSIBILITIES
Project Sheets

Styrofoam™ **plastic foam** is easy to cut, sand, paint, and glue, making it ideal for arts and crafts projects at school and at home. Create a variety of useful household items and zany critters with a set of **FREE project sheets** from Dow Chemical. You'll get instructions and supplies lists on how to make a sports or tennis shoe cornice, finger puppets, dinosaurs, cookie cutter crafts, and creepy crawlies.

Phone: 1-888-462-7238

Ask For: Styrofoam Project Sheets

Web Site: www.styrofoam-crafts.com

DIFF'RENT STROKES
Painting Guide and Project Sheets

Fire up the imagination of your students—and yourself—with **four project sheets** that show you how to give everyday items a new look with **acrylic paints**. Add pizzazz to wooden trays, create a Bavarian folk art checkbook cover, turn a wooden chair into a bold masterpiece, and give picture frames a colorful makeover. You also receive a brochure, "The Basics of Decorative Painting," which details four basic brush strokes: the comma stroke, the teardrop stroke, the C-stroke, and the S-stroke.

> **Send:** LSASE
>
> **Ask For:** "Basics of Decorative Painting" & Four Project Sheets
>
> **Mail To:** Delta Technical Coatings
> Dept. FTE
> 2550 Pellissier Place
> Whittier, CA 90601-1505

IT'S A SCRAP
Scrapbook Supplies Catalog

Before your students take on a scrapbook project, peruse through the StarMaster **scrapbook supplies catalog** for sticker and stationery offers and other decorative ideas that add snap to scrapbooks. With this offer you also receive two colorful, acid-free die-cut shapes that can be pasted into a scrapbook right away.

> **Send:** LSASE with 25¢ and two first-class stamps affixed
>
> **Ask For:** Die-cut Shapes & StarMaster Catalog
>
> **Mail To:** Detra Tolman
> StarMaster
> 2500 Laurelhill Lane
> Ft. Worth, TX 76133-8112

GETTING TO THE POINT
Sewing Brochure

Looking for a way to manage everyday stress and strain? Engage in the leisure-time activity of sewing! A study commissioned by the American Home Sewing & Craft Association revealed that this beloved hobby has stress-relieving benefits. In the study, both experienced and beginner sewers showed reduced heart rate and blood pressure while engaged in the activity. Read more about this antidote to stress in **"It's Sew Soothing,"** an informative **brochure**.

> **Send:** LSASE
> **Ask For:** "Sewing . . . It's Sew Soothing"
> **Mail To:** Home Sewing Association
> 1350 Broadway, Ste. 1601
> New York, NY 10018

POTPOURRI POWER
Sachet Bag Kit

Fill your room with fragrant potpourri with a set of two pairs of **precut sachet bags**. Just stitch them together and stuff with your favorite potpourri, scented cotton balls, sweet-smelling herbs, or fragrant pine needles to make a bag for yourself and one to give as a scent-sational gift. If you like, tie a ribbon around the finished bag, make a bow, and glue on a flower for a special touch.

> **Send:** $1.50 P&H
> **Ask For:** Precut Sachet Bag Kit
> **Mail To:** Taylor's Cutaways & Stuff
> 2802 E. Washington St.
> Urbana, IL 61802-4660
> **Web Site:** home.sprynet.com/sprynet/tcutaway

USE YOUR HEAD
Indian Headdress Kit

Now students can make a decorative replica of an Indian headdress, a famous Native American symbol. With this **Indian chief's headdress kit,** which includes safety pins, feathers, wire, hanging line, and faceted colored beads, you'll have everything you need to create a colorful 3" x 5" headdress. Easy-to-follow instructions are also included.

Send: $2.25 P&H
Ask For: Indian Chief's Headdress Kit
Mail To: Creative Corner
P.O. Box 1361
Apple Valley, CA 92307

SPOOL-ISH PLEASURES
Tree Ornament Kit

Here's a "tree"-mendous addition to your classroom Christmas tree. This unusual little **ornament** is a Christmas tree made of miniature spools. The kit comes with 16 wooden spools, colorful fabric to cover the spools, and a loop of thread for hanging. Use your own fabric swatches to create an ornament that is appropriate year-round, not just during the holidays. The ornament also can be purchased fully assembled.

Send: $1.25 P&H for kit; $2.00 fully assembled
Ask For: Spool Tree Kit or Ornament
Mail To: Lynette's Attic
P.O. Box 0002
Grover, PA 17735

PLAY CLAY
Instructional Brochure

With just baking soda, cornstarch, water, and food coloring, students can make **Play Clay** and create a variety of colorful crafts, including jewelry, holiday decorations, and sculpted animals. This homemade modeling clay becomes permanent after drying and is suitable for all ages. Send for a **FREE brochure** that contains the Play Clay recipe and instructions for crafting picture frames, coasters, hair barrettes, and more.

Send: LSASE
Ask For: "Play Clay"
Mail To: "Play Clay"
P.O. Box 7468
Princeton, NJ 08540

HELLO, DOLLY!
Spool Doll Kit

Perfect for a decoration or an addition to a doll collection, this **spool doll kit** contains simple instructions on how to make a country doll that is 6" tall. The kit comes with mini wooden spools, jute, yarn, fabric, and ribbon. Just provide a glue gun, scissors, and needle and thread to fashion a new little friend.

Send: $2.00 P&H
Ask For: Spool Doll Kit
Mail To: The Wren's Nest
6220 Neubert Springs Rd.
Knoxville, TN 37920

Food & Drink

Recipe Booklet

"The Secrets to Great Popcorn" is a **FREE booklet** from Whirley-Pop, makers of the original hand-crank popping machine. The booklet contains step-by-step popping directions, clean-up tips, and nutrition information. Cheddar Bacon Popcorn, Reggae Popcorn, and Maple Popcorn are among the recipes included.

Send: Your name & address
Ask For: Recipe Booklet
Mail To: Wabash Valley Farms
P.O. Box 715
Monon, IN 47959

Recipe Leaflet

Let Land O' Lakes give you ideas for scrumptious holiday treats and quick baking tips. Expert home economists will answer your questions on baking during November and December, and in addition you receive a **FREE recipe leaflet, "Land O' Lakes Bakes You a Star."** One year the experts at the Land O' Lakes Holiday Bakeline helped 55,000 callers. Join the fun!

Phone: 1-800-782-9606
Ask For: "Land O' Lakes Bakes You a Star"
Limit: One per household
Web Site: www.landolakes.com

NO PLACE LIKE HOME COOKING
Baby Food Booklet

Commercial baby foods are overpriced and overloaded with water, thickeners, chemicals, and sugars, according to the Center for Science in the Public Interest. Yet most parents continue to feed store-bought foods to their infants. Learn how to safely clean, prepare, store, and reheat your own nutritious baby foods with **"Super Baby Food."** All you need is this 50-page **booklet** and a food processor or blender, and you're on your way to saving more than $300 a year on baby food.

Send: $2.00 P&H
Ask For: "Super Baby Food"
Mail To: F. J. Roberts Publishing
900 Henry St.
Archbald, PA 18403
Web Site: www.superbabyfood.com

FRY ONE ON
Recipe Booklet

For a year's worth of great cooking ideas, turn to a **FREE booklet, "Recipe News You Can Use."** This handy collection of 12 tasty recipes—one for every month—comes from the makers of French's French Fried Onions. Each dish can be made in 20 minutes or less and contains only a few steps. Also included is a coupon for your next purchase of French's Onions.

Send: Your name & address
Ask For: "Recipe News You Can Use"
Mail To: French's French Fried Onions
P.O. Box 6853
Young America, MN 55558-6853

THE MAIN SQUEEZE
Lemon Recipe Booklet

Any way you slice it, lemons really enhance the flavor of fish and seafood. With this **FREE booklet,** you learn ways to cook fish using lemons, as well as tips on buying lemons and fresh fish. The booklet also includes a number of fabulous recipes, including Lemon-Herbed Seafood Kabobs, Salmon Balls with Lemon-Mustard Sauce, and Lemony Fresh Tartar Sauce.

Send: LSASE
Ask For: "How to Better Fish"
Mail To: Office of Consumer Affairs
P.O. Box 7888
Van Nuys, CA 91409-7888

FOR KIDS ONLY
Popcorn Recipe and Crafts Brochure

Kids have unique ideas about what they like to do and what they like to eat. These ideas have been incorporated into a **brochure, "Popcorn Recipes and Crafts For Kids Only."** The activities are simple enough to handle alone but are more fun if the entire family is involved. The brochure contains recipes (ReciPops) and crafts (Pop Arts 'N Crafts) for each season of the year and is filled with popcorn trivia and tips to fire up any child's imagination.

Send: 75¢ P&H or UPC/proof of purchase
Ask For: Jolly Time Popcorn "For Kids Only" Brochure
Mail To: Jolly Time
Dept. FB, P.O. Box 178
Sioux City, IA 51102
Web Site: www.jollytime.com

GOURMET GRILLING
Recipe Booklet

Summertime or almost anytime of the year, grilling is a favorite outdoor activity all over the country. With Broilmaster's **FREE recipe booklet, "The Juiciest Recipes Known to Man,"** you learn how to cook up Glazed Salmon Supreme, Caliente Chili-Rubbed Steaks, Spicy Spitfire Chicken, and other mouth-watering dishes. Broilmaster gas grills are also ideal for baking, steaming, broiling, and sautéing.

Send:	Your name & address
Ask For:	"The Juiciest Recipes Known to Man"
Mail To:	Broilmaster Premium Gas Grills
	P.O. Box 128
	Florence, AL 35631
Limit:	One per person
Web Site:	www.broilmaster.com

DINNERTIME SURVIVAL
Recipe Booklet

If you're constantly on the move, cooking interesting gourmet meals at home need not be as time-consuming as you might think. A **FREE booklet, "Dinnertime Survival,"** from the California Olive Industry, contains recipes that use shortcuts and quick-fix ingredients. In addition to showing you how to put together such tempting dishes as Deep-Dish Tortilla Pie and Pasta Pensacola in a snap, the booklet provides helpful equipment tips, trade secrets, and shortcuts for special occasions.

Send:	Your name & address
Ask For:	"Dinnertime Survival"
Mail To:	California Olive Industry
	Dept. DSF
	P.O. Box 7796
	Fresno, CA 93747

HEAL THYSELF
Catalog and Tea Sample

Natural herbs are known for their rejuvenating healing powers. The Indiana Botanic Gardens is offering a current **catalog** of more than 500 different herbs, teas, and other products prepared from all-natural ingredients, as well as guides on herbal remedies. Also included is a sample of the company's best-selling **Sausalito Spice Tea,** a soothing blend of cinnamon, orange peel, cloves, allspice, ginger, cardamom, and fennel.

Send: $1.00 P&H

Ask For: Tea Bag & Catalog

Mail To: Indiana Botanic Gardens
Dept. FB9AB
3401 W. 37th Ave.
Hobart, IN 46342

TOTALLY HOT
Spicy Nuts Sample

You'll go nuts over this **sample of hot and spicy nuts.** They're great for snacking, for serving at parties, and just about anytime you've got a hankering for something hot. Nuts are also a good source of protein. Send for your 1.5-ounce sample bag today.

Send: $1.25 P&H

Ask For: 1.5-ounce bag of Hot Spicy Nuts

Mail To: Richard's Spicy Nuts
P.O. Box 1208
Alturas, CA 96101-1208

OAT TO JOY
Brochure

Did you know that hot oatmeal costs less than 15 cents a serving? Or that oatmeal has orbited the Earth with the U.S. astronauts? Find out historic and nutritional facts about oats, along with the differences between old-fashioned oats, steel-cut oats, and quick oats, in **"Oats: The Whole (Grain) Story."** This **FREE brochure** also traces the grain from farm to mill to market and has ideas for tasty oatmeal toppings and recipes.

Send: Your name & address
Ask For: "Oats: The Whole (Grain) Story"
Mail To: "Oats: The Whole (Grain) Story"
P.O. Box 487, Dept. F
Chicago, IL 60690-0487

WHOLE LOTTA SHAKIN'
Recipe Club Newsletter

Get the scoop on healthier, more creative cooking and eating ideas with **"What's Shaking,"** a **FREE newsletter** dedicated to providing handy, healthful cooking and food preparation tips, such as substituting tofu for half the eggs in egg salad and making a quick vinaigrette out of apple cider vinegar, olive or vegetable oil, and seasonings. You also get recipes, coupons, letters from readers, and nutritional facts, plus information on how to join the recipe club.

Phone: 1-800-622-DASH (622-3274)
Ask For: Recipe Club Newsletter with Recipes & Coupons

LEGGO MY LEGUME
Recipe Pamphlets

Legumes—dry peas, lentils, and chickpeas—can be cooked in a variety of appealing ways and make great accompaniments for pasta, fish, fowl, and meat. Plus, they're rich in folate, which helps prevent arteriosclerosis and heart disease. **Two FREE pamphlets** contain important nutritional information on this vitamin, along with delicious recipes for creating Italian Pea Soup, Legume Sauerkraut Salad, Pasta Sauce with Lentils, and yes, even Lemony Chickpea Cake!

Send: LSASE
Ask For: Recipes & Info
Mail To: USA Dry Pea & Lentil Council
5071 Hwy. 8 West
Moscow, ID 83843-4023

ORANGE YOU GLAD?
Booklet

Did you know that eating just one orange gives you 130 percent daily value for vitamin C, 28 percent daily value for fiber, and 12 percent daily value for folic acid? They are fat free, cholesterol free, and at only 70 calories, oranges are a healthful, nutritious food. Vitamin C improves your immune system, acts as a powerful antioxidant, and reduces your risk for certain types of cancer. Get the nutritional lowdown from this **FREE brochure**.

Send: LSASE
Ask For: "Just One"
Mail To: Office of Consumer Affairs
P.O. Box 7888
Van Nuys, CA 91409-7888

RICE 'N' EASY
Recipe Brochure

If you're looking for ways to make cooking rice dishes faster, easier, and more fun, this **FREE brochure** from the USA Rice Council should do the trick. **"Rice Tricks"** teaches you how to whip up Cowboy Rice and Beans, Ten-Minute Turkey Teriyaki, Crustless Creamy Chicken Pot Pie, and other gourmet grain dishes, accentuated with various stir-in tricks, storage tricks, international tricks, and quick-trick meals.

Send: LSASE
Ask For: "Rice Tricks" Booklet
Mail To: Rice Tricks c/o USA Rice Council
P.O. Box 740121
Houston, TX 77274

QUITE A DISH
Chicken Recipes

For today's busy cook, one-dish meals are a lifesaver. They're easy to make and provide all the ingredients and nutrition of a complete meal. **"One-Dish Chicken Dinners"** is a **FREE brochure** filled with creative recipes that can be made in a single stove-top skillet or oven-to-table casserole dish. Treat your friends or family to Cran-Apple Chicken and Rice, North African Chicken with Couscous, Fiesta Chicken Stew with Cornbread Dumplings, Pan-Roasted Chicken and Vegetables, and other delicious offerings.

Send: LSASE
Ask For: "One-Dish Dinners"
Mail To: One-Dish Dinners (FBT)
c/o Delmarva Poultry
R.D. 6, Box 47
Georgetown, DE 19947-9575

A PASSION FOR PEARS
Recipe Booklet

Pears from the Pacific Northwest make great additions to everything from simple salads to elegant desserts. And because they're canned, you don't need to worry about ripening, peeling, or cutting. Among the tantalizing dishes you can make are Yakima Valley Pear-Berry Cobbler, Fraser River Salmon Bake, and Oregon Bay Shrimp and Pear Salad. Send for a **FREE recipe brochure** today.

> **Send:** LSASE
> **Ask For:** "Always Ripe, Always Ready" recipe brochure
> **Mail To:** Pacific Northwest Canned Pears
> Dept. FREE
> 105 S. 18th St., Ste. 205
> Yakima, WA 98901-2149

KNOWING THE EGG-SENTIALS
Cholesterol Education Pamphlet

Following a cholesterol-conscious program involves choosing a variety of foods that are low in saturated fat and include the proper amounts of vegetables, fruits, and grains. But that doesn't mean you have to give up your favorite foods. **"Cholesterol-Conscious Cooking with Eggs"** is aimed at health-conscious consumers who want to know how to include eggs in a healthful diet. This **FREE booklet** features a five-day suggested menu plan and five recipes, including a one-dish pizza, a crab omelette, and a French toast strata. A coupon is also included.

> **Send:** LSASE
> **Ask For:** Brochure plus coupon
> **Mail To:** Eggland's Best, Inc.
> 842 First Ave.
> King of Prussia, PA 19406-1404
> **Limit:** One per customer

Seeds and Catalog

When it comes to making gourmet meals out of the freshest seasonings, you can't get any fresher than straight from your garden to your kitchen. With **five seed packets** containing caraway, chervil, dill, basil, and chives, you can start your own herb garden. Easy-to-follow planting instructions are included, and you also receive a **catalog** of other seeds and gourmet supplies—such as shallots, ginseng, and Egyptian onions—and recipes for using your homegrown herbs.

Send: $1.00 P&H
Ask For: Herb Seed Sampler
Mail To: Le Jardin du Gourmet
P.O. Box 75D
St. Johnsbury Center, VT 05863

Informational Booklet

Welcome to the world of the fresh lemon. From the history of the lemon to its proper selection, storage, preparation, and serving, a **FREE booklet** fills you in on how to enjoy the benefits of this sunny citrus. **"150 Ways to Use a Fresh Lemon"** is packed with more than a hundred tips on perking up beverages, decorations and garnishes, desserts, fish and seafood, fruits, meats, pasta, rice, salads, soups, appetizers, and vegetables. You also get hints on how to use lemon juice and lemon peels in household cleaning and deodorizing.

Send: LSASE
Ask For: "150 Ways to Use a Fresh Lemon"
Mail To: Office of Consumer Affairs
P.O. Box 7888
Van Nuys, CA 91409-7888

At Home

Home Maintenance Checklist

Like people, homes need regular checkups, too. When was the last time you surveyed your household for potential leaks, cracks in retaining walls, dry rot, insect infestation, and damaged or missing roof shingles? Inspect your home on a regular basis with a **preventive maintenance guide and checklist** from HouseMaster, a national home inspection company. This guide shows even the novice homeowner where potential problems may lie and how to detect them.

> **Send:** LSASE
> **Ask For:** Home Maintenance Checklist
> **Mail To:** HouseMaster Home Maintenance Checklist
> 421 W. Union Ave.
> Bound Brook, NJ 08805

Tomato Plants

When it comes to adding snap to salads, salsa, and hamburgers, nothing tastes as good as succulent home-grown tomatoes. With the **Big Red Tomato Starter Kit,** students can grow more than six plants that produce up to 100 pounds of plump Miracle Sweet tomatoes. The tomato-shaped kit includes seeds, potting mix, two growing containers, and instructions for cultivating a 10' plant. Maturity is about 67 days from transplanting, and each fruit should weigh about 5 to 6 ounces.

> **Send:** $2.25 P&H
> **Ask For:** Big Red Tomato Starter Kit
> **Mail To:** Big Red Tomato
> P.O. Box 3498
> San Rafael, CA 94912-3498

BABY MINE
Crib Safety Brochure

"Is Your Baby Safe?" is a **brochure** that addresses the utmost concern to new parents in selecting baby furniture. This checklist informs parents what to look for when selecting a crib for their child. It's something no parent of a newborn should be without.

> **Send:** LSASE
> **Ask For:** "Is Your Baby Safe?" Brochure
> **Mail To:** The Danny Foundation
> 3158 Danville Blvd.
> Alamo, CA 94507
> **Web Site:** www.dannyfoundation.org

REFRIGERATOR ROUNDUP
Brochure

On cleaning day, are you afraid to face the fridge? You may be suffering from fridgeaphobia. Whirlpool is issuing a **FREE brochure** to help you conquer your fear and tackle that refrigerator with fervor. You'll get tips on how to spot and eliminate USOs—food items that have evolved into new life-forms—clean out the inside of your refrigerator properly, and remove those pesky, lingering odors. The humorous guide also includes recipes and maximum shelf times for leftovers.

> **Send:** LSASE
> **Ask For:** "Clean Out Your Refrigerator" brochure
> **Mail To:** Whirlpool Clean Out Your Refrigerator Day
> 43 N. Canal
> Chicago, IL 60606

GREEN THUMB
Greenhouse Kit

Open a window on learning with this **greenhouse kit,** complete with potting mix, 7" x 9" x 2" greenhouse, and more than 50 seeds for growing chives and thyme. After the seeds are planted, simply add water, close up the greenhouse, place it on a windowsill, and watch the results. When the plants reach 6" high, they can be transplanted to a pot.

Send: $2.00 P&H
Ask For: Greenhouse Kit
Mail To: Greenhouse
P.O. Box 3595
San Rafael, CA 94902

HOME IS WHERE THE HEARTH IS
Heating Products Guide

On those cold, blustery days, you want a heating system that provides warmth evenly throughout your home, leaving no cold pockets or hot zones. Silent, odor-free, and almost four times more economical than electricity, gas delivers heat efficiently for pennies an hour. A line of heating products for the home, from gas fireplaces and stoves to room heaters, is described in a **FREE** 24-page **hearth and heating pocket guide**.

Send: Your name & address
Ask For: Hearth & Heating Pocket Guide
Mail To: Martin Gas Products
P.O. Box 128
Florence, AL 35631
Limit: One per household

WOODEN IT BE NICE?
Wood Care Brochure

Just like skin, wood contains "pores" that allow it to "breathe." When these pores become clogged with dust and other contaminants, the finish may crack, flake, or peel. **"Caring for Fine Wood"** is a **brochure** that outlines a three-step system for cleansing, moisturizing, and protecting wood furniture from pollution, sunlight, humidity, and silicone, the most common threats. Help your family heirlooms and your new fine-wood furniture purchases breathe easier by giving them the "spa" treatment.

Send: LSASE
Ask For: "Caring for Fine Wood"
Mail To: Weiman Furniture Care
P.O. Box 9569
Downers Grove, IL 60515

SUCCULENT SAGUARO
Cactus Seeds

No wonder it's called "king of the cacti." Fully grown, the giant saguaro has been known to reach 40' tall, weigh 9 tons, and live for more than 200 years. Start your own "saguaro city" with a packet of 100 **saguaro seeds**. Follow the instructions and your seeds should sprout in about two weeks. In six to nine months, the cacti should be ½" high.

Send: $1.00 P&H
Ask For: Saguaro Seeds
Mail To: Cactus Club of Arizona, Inc.
12629 N. Tatum Blvd., #524
Phoenix, AZ 85032

SOAKING IT UP
Plant Coaster

Does your pot runneth over every time you overwater your plants? Prevent the mess from spilling onto the furniture or floor with the **Miracle Plant Coaster**. This 8" circular disc absorbs more than eight times its weight in water to protect whatever surface it covers. Made of 100 percent acrylic with a waterproof vinyl backing, this handy coaster dries quickly and is also mildew resistant and machine washable.

Send: $1.75 P&H
Ask For: Plant Coaster
Mail To: RPM
Pentagon Towers
P.O. Box 36083
Minneapolis, MN 55435
Limit: Two per household

IT'S A TOSS-UP
Salad Garden Seed Mix

Summertime or anytime, there's nothing as refreshing as a cool, crisp salad with all the fixings. Fresh from your backyard to your dining room table, you can cultivate the ingredients for a healthy, colorful concoction with a **salad garden seed mix**. With each order you receive a packet of Danvers Carrots and a packet of Romaine Lettuce seeds.

Send: $1.00 P&H
Ask For: Salad Garden Seeds
Mail To: Butterbrooke Farm
78 Barry Rd.
Oxford, CT 06478

IN THE MODE
Fashion Advice

When applying for a job, having the right wardrobe is important in making a good first impression. Limited budgets, confusion over dress codes, and diverse fabric options make choosing a wardrobe a challenge. The Woolite Fashion Forum's **FREE fashion report** gives practical advice for women on the purchase and care of business attire. The report describes how to familiarize yourself with fabrics and work within your budget, among other tips.

Send: Your name & address
Ask For: Woolite Fashion Forum Report
Mail To: Woolite Fashion Forum Report
P.O. Box 1197
Grand Rapids, MN 55745-1197

WHAT'S THE HOLDUP?
Memo Holder

Shopping List
Milk
Eggs
Bread
Cereal

Keep those reminders in sight with this cute **teddy bear memo holder**. This handcrafted wooden helper measures about 4" long and has a magnetic strip on the back for use on the refrigerator or other prominent surface. Great for holding up shopping lists, notes, memos, photos, report cards, and more.

Send: $1.50 P&H
Ask For: Teddy Bear Magnet
Mail To: JoAnn's Crafts
131 Crocker Drive
Mooresboro, NC 28114

GLASS AND GLASNOST
Miniature Animals

Lovers of miniatures will take a big interest in these charming little critters. Handcrafted in Russia, these **tiny glass animals,** each measuring less than 1" long, are a collector's treasure. Fifteen different creatures are available (supplier's choice), including a cat, dog, cow, penguin, rabbit, goose, and fish.

Send: $2.00 P&H for one
Ask For: Mini Glass Animal
Mail To: Lea Zengaqe
13721 12th St. NE
Lake Stevens, WA 98258

RAISING TODAY'S TEENS
Helpline and Publication

Parenting a teen can be difficult. "The key to success," says Sue Kauffman, founder of the Marion Foundation, which seeks to foster relationships among students, parents, and educators through innovative programs, "is helping parents communicate more effectively with their teen." That's why the foundation established a **support network for parents** called **Raising Today's Teens.** Through a **toll-free helpline and Web site,** parents can get private, one-on-one counseling. Complementing the program is a **publication** that features insightful articles written by professionals, parents, and teens themselves.

Phone: 1-800-475-TALK (475-8255)
Ask For: "Raising Today's Teens"
Web Site: www.raisingtodaysteens.org

IN CASE OF EMERGENCY
Fire Pail Instructions

If a cooking fire or electrical fire broke out in your home, would you know what to do? Send for a set of **emergency fire pail instructions** and learn how to make an extinguisher out of an empty one-pound coffee can. Craft a handle out of spools, corks, beads, clothespins, or ice-cream sticks, attach it to the can with wire, and fill with baking soda. Keep a pail handy on camping trips, in the laundry room, in the garage, and other areas where small fires most often occur. (This homemade extinguisher is not meant to replace your home's commercial fire extinguisher.)

Send: LSASE

Ask For: Emergency Fire Pail Instructions

Mail To: Emergency Fire Pail Instructions
P.O. Box 7468
Princeton, NJ 08540

POSTER-HASTE
Movie Poster

Hollywood is hot! Collecting movie memorabilia is more popular than ever. Movie posters often sell for thousands at auction. Fortunately, *FREEBIES* readers can receive a full-color **movie poster** (supplier's choice) for only $2.00 from Studio Archives, run by television producer and talent coordinator Len Miller. Supplied by major film studios, the one-sheet poster measures 26" x 40" and is an original lithograph that has never been used.

Send: $2.00 P&H

Ask For: Movie Poster

Mail To: Studio-A
1900 Vine St., #315
Hollywood, CA 90068

Limit: Five per inquiry

MORE THAN JUST FUN AND GAMES

Toy Safety Booklet

Children's playtime is also a time for learning to solve problems, fostering creativity, developing leadership skills, and getting along with others. The Toy Manufacturers of America has put together **"Toys & Play,"** a **FREE toy safety and selection booklet**. The 24-page publication tells parents how to choose safe, age-appropriate toys, emphasizes proper supervision, and advises how to help youngsters get the most out of playtime. A toy buying guide is also included. The booklet is available in Spanish.

Send: Your name & address

Ask For: "TMA Guide to Toys & Play" (please specify English or Spanish)

Mail To: Toy Booklet
P.O. Box 866
Madison Square Station
New York, NY 10159-0866

GIFT IDEAS

Favorite Gifts Catalog

The next time a child's birthday or another special occasion is coming up and you're too busy to shop, turn to "Favorite Gifts." This **FREE catalog** features earth-sensitive and educational toys, books, and puzzles for kids. It's a lifesaver for working parents and grandparents. Take advantage of the **FREE birthday reminder service** by filling out the form in the catalog. You will be reminded three to four weeks before the occasion and provided with great gift suggestions.

Phone: 1-800-528-5333

Ask For: Favorite Gifts Catalog

Web Site: www.favgifts.com

WRITES OF SPRING
Notecards

Is spring bringing thoughts of love and romance? Express your poetry or heartfelt sentiments to that special someone on these **"Appalachian Wilds" notecards**. You get four 4¼" x 5½" notecards printed on quality card stock with coordinating envelopes. Each card features a pen-and-ink drawing of an Appalachian wildflower. A rose-and-lavender sachet is included with each package as well.

Send: $1.50 P&H

Ask For: Spring Notecards

Mail To: The Wren's Nest
6220 Neubert Springs Rd.
Knoxville, TN 37920

SAFETY STARTS AT HOME
Deputy Fire Marshal Kit

Every home should have a fire escape plan. For help in establishing one, consult your local fire station for advice. Teach the plan to your children, rehearse it, and familiarize your youngsters with your home's smoke detectors. Send for this **FREE Deputy Fire Marshal Kit,** which includes stickers, a badge, and an ID card. Aimed at elementary-age children, the kit also includes a certificate indicating that the bearer has learned the "cool rules" of fire safety, including "stop, drop, and roll" and knowing local emergency numbers.

Send: Your name & address

Ask For: Deputy Fire Marshal Kit

Mail To: National Consumers League
1701 K St. NW, Ste. 1200
Washington, DC 20006

WHAT, ME WORRY?
Worry Dolls

The highland Indians of Guatemala believe that if you share your problems with a worry doll, the doll will take your worries away. Test the legend for yourself with a set of **Guatemalan worry dolls**. You receive six colorful handcrafted dolls, each measuring 1" long. The dolls come in a fabric pouch with a drawstring closure that doubles as a necklace. A copy of the "worry doll legend" is also included.

Send: $2.00 P&H
Ask For: Worry Dolls
Mail To: Mostly Art
P.O. Box 24725
Denver, CO 80224-0725

COUPON CHIC
Coupon Organizer

Using coupons at the grocery store saves money, but handling all those clipped pieces of paper can get unwieldy. This handy **coupon keeper** helps you organize and separate hundreds of coupons by type using labeled index cards. Made of washable nylon, this 5" x 8" pouch has a Velcro® closure and can expand to more than 2" thick. The pouch comes in a variety of colors (supplier's choice).

Send: $1.00 P&H
Ask For: Coupon Organizer
Mail To: Diamond
Dept. F
P.O. Box 184
George, IA 51237-0184

A HOUSEFUL OF USES
Brochure

Baking soda is useful in more than just cooking; it's good for a variety of household cleansing, personal care, and deodorizing applications. A **FREE brochure** from Arm & Hammer provides a room-by-room user's guide for this economic, environmentally safe product. In the family room, for instance, baking soda cleans scuff marks and upholstery and deodorizes ashtrays and carpets. In the bathroom, you can use baking soda as a bath additive, mouthwash, and body deodorant.

Send: LSASE
Ask For: "A House-full of Uses"
Mail To: "A House-full of Uses"
P.O. Box 7468
Princeton, NJ 08540

GOOD MOOS
Cow Paper Garland

Good moos for all the cow lovers out there. With this offer, you receive decorative **cow garland,** featuring a black-and-white cow with a red ribbon around her neck. The 8' paper garland is ideal for dressing up a farm display or to add some creative fun to any occasion.

Send: $1.50 P&H
Ask For: Cow Paper Garland
Mail To: Kaye's Holiday—Dept. CG
6N021 Meredith Rd.
Maple Park, IL 60151

Health & Beauty

Brochure

A natural aid for health and grooming, baking soda is a versatile, safe, and economical product that dissolves oils, grease, and dirt. Learn fun facts about your skin, the proper care of hands and feet, the right way to shampoo, and how to protect your teeth and gums with a **FREE brochure, "Looking Good Is a Natural."**

Send: LSASE

Ask For: "Looking Good Is a Natural"

Mail To: "Looking Good Is a Natural"
P.O. Box 7468
Princeton, NJ 08540

Brochures

The Baylor College of Medicine is offering a series of **FREE brochures** on important health issues women face throughout their lives. Choose from these titles:

"Vitality, Vim & Vigor: Six Steps to More Energy"

"Blood Pressure: Take Control"

"Your Back: An Owner's Manual"

"Diabetes" (also available in Spanish)

"Living with Asthma"

"Women's Health: Ideas for a Lifetime of Wellness"

"Accident Prevention: A Family Guide to Child Safety"
(also available in Spanish)

"Es Hora de Comer!"

Send: LSASE for each brochure

Ask For: Please specify brochure by title

Mail To: We Care For You
Baylor College of Medicine
Houston, TX 77030

HEART TO HEART
Health Information

From eating right to exercising properly to knowing your cholesterol level, blood pressure, and family history, practicing a heart-healthy lifestyle holds benefits for everyone. Get on the road to health and well-being with **"HeartScan's Top Tips for Heart Healthy Living,"** developed by Imatron, creators of the UltraFast CT Scanner for early detection of heart disease, and by HeartScan, the nationwide network of coronary disease risk-assessment centers. Visit the Web site below for more information.

Phone: 1-800-469-HEART
Ask For: UltraFast CT Scanner & HeartScan Tips
Web Site: www.HeartScan.com

HOME, SNEEZE HOME?
Brochure

If you wake up almost every morning with a stuffy nose and watery eyes, you may be allergic to your own home! The problem may lie with your pillow, your plants, or your pets. More than half the 35 million allergy sufferers are allergic to indoor allergens, such as dust mites, pet dander, and mold spores. Send for a **FREE newsletter, "Are You Allergic to Your Home?"** and find out how to avoid and reduce your exposure to indoor allergens.

Send: LSASE
Ask For: Indoor Allergy Newsletter
Mail To: Wina Products, Inc.
P.O. 320571
Fairfield, CT 06432

ITCHING FOR INFORMATION
Newsletter

Whether it's mosquitoes and poison ivy in the summer or skin-drying, low humidity temperatures in the winter, you probably have an itch to scratch all year round. Learn fun facts about skin, how to take care of your skin, and how to avoid and relieve seasonal itching with a **FREE sample of *The Itch Inquirer* newsletter**. You receive either fall/winter or spring/summer information, depending on the season.

Send: LSASE

Ask For: Itch Newsletter

Mail To: Lanacane Itch Information Center
P.O. Box 328-LC
White Plains, NY 10602-0328

IN-SIGHTFUL INFORMATION
Vision Brochure

Our eyes are perhaps our most treasured of the five senses. The National Society to Prevent Blindness has published an informative **FREE brochure** to help educate students about the anatomy of the eye, the eye-brain connection, and how vision works. Eye protection tips and important vocabulary words are also featured in **"The Eye and How We See."** Download vision tests, coloring sheets, and other information off the organization's Web site.

Phone: 1-800-331-2020
or

Send: Your name & address

Ask For: "The Eye and How We See"

Mail To: Prevent Blindness America
500 E. Remington Rd.
Schaumburg, IL 60173

Web Site: www.preventblindness.org

THAT CERTAIN SMILE
Cosmetic Dentistry Information

From the *Mona Lisa* to the model on a fashion magazine cover, the smile has carried much significance as an indication of an individual's sense of well-being. In a survey, more than 92 percent of adults agreed that an attractive smile is an important social asset, and nearly half said they would like to improve how their smile looks, whether it's correcting gapped or crooked teeth or fixing cracked or worn-down teeth. **"Your Smile Says It All"** outlines dental problems and cosmetic dentistry solutions and guides you in choosing an experienced professional. The **FREE brochure** is published by the American Academy of Cosmetic Dentistry.

> **Send:** Your name & address
> **Ask For:** "Your Smile Says It All"
> **Mail To:** AACD
> 270 Corporate Dr., Dept. F
> Madison, WI 53714

GOOD HAIR DAY
Hair Tie

You won't pull your hair out with a **Crunchie hair tie**. Crunchies are made of soft fleece so they won't slip off or tear out your hair like some other hair accessories do. Crunchies come in a variety of fashionable colors and are washable, too. With this offer you get one solid-color crunchie (supplier's choice).

> **Send:** $1.00 P&H
> **Ask For:** Crunchie
> **Mail To:** Christine's
> 7808 N. Cedar Way
> Park City, UT 84098-5176
> **Limit:** One per household

NOW EAR THIS
Christmas Earrings

Christmas is a special time of year, one for gatherings and reunions with family and friends. This holiday season, brighten up your wardrobe with a pair of adorable **Christmas earrings**. The jewelry comes in a variety of styles (supplier's choice), such as red-and-white striped candy canes tied with a gold bow.

Send: $1.00 P&H for two
Ask For: Christmas Earrings
Mail To: McVehil's Mercantile
Three Rasel Ave., Dept. FBER
Washington, PA 15301-7120

STRAIGHT TALK ABOUT MENTAL ILLNESS
Pamphlet Series

"Let's Talk Facts About Mental Illness" is a **FREE 19-pamphlet series** published by the American Psychiatric Association in an outreach effort to educate the community at large. Ideal as a supplement to your classroom health curriculum, the series covers a wide range of relevant topics, including childhood disorders, teen suicide, eating disorders, bipolar disorder, depression, coping with HIV and AIDS, substance abuse, panic disorders, obsessive-compulsive disorder, psychotherapy, and phobias.

Send: Your name & address
Ask For: "Let's Talk Facts" series
Mail To: American Psychiatric Association
Public Affairs, Dept. FFN-T
1400 K St. NW
Washington, DC 20005
Limit: One series per address

EYE CARE FOR SENIORS
Brochure

By age 65, one out of three Americans has some form of vision-threatening eye disease such as glaucoma, cataracts, and macular degeneration. Some older Americans aren't aware they're at risk or can't afford to pay for care. The National Eye Care Project is a public service outreach program that provides medical eye care for financially disadvantaged seniors. Callers to the toll-free number receive a **FREE brochure** and, pending eligibility, are matched with a volunteer ophthalmologist.

Phone: 1-800-222-EYES (3937)
Ask For: "Sight-Saving Care for the Elderly" brochure

MILES FOR HEALTH
Club Membership Offer

The **U.S. 100 Mile Club** was established to motivate people to get involved in physical fitness, and to reward them for the amount that they exercise. For every 10 minutes of vigorous exercise or actual mileage, members receive one mile. The 100 miles can be accumulated through any type of physical activity. Once your miles have been transmitted, you receive a copy of the club's annual newsletter and a certificate of athletic achievement. With this offer you receive a membership entry form and a **patch** sporting the club's logo, an eagle flying in front of the American flag.

Send: $2.00 P&H plus LSASE
Ask For: Logo Patch
Mail To: Dart Enterprises
P.O. Box 1208
Alturas, CA 96101

EYE ON HOME SAFETY
Safety Guide

Is your home hazardous to your family's eyes? Find out how safe your household habits are with the **"Home Eye Safety Guide"** from the National Society to Prevent Blindness. This **publication** tests you on how you handle cleaning products, your yard and garden habits, the toy and play areas in your home, your family's sports safety practices, whether you maintain a safe home workshop, your driving and car maintenance habits, and the possible hazards around your home. Suggestions for protective eyewear are also included. Download vision tests, coloring sheets, and other information off the organization's Web site.

Phone: 1-800-331-2020

or

Send: Your name & address

Ask For: Home Eye Safety Guide

Mail To: Prevent Blindness America
500 E. Remington Rd.
Schaumburg, IL 60173

Web Site: www.preventblindness.org

EAR'S THE THING
Fimo Bead Earrings

Suitable for any occasion, these ½" **Fimo bead earrings** are crafted out of colorful Fimo clay on surgical steel French hook wires. The artsy, handmade earrings come in a variety of designs and colors (supplier's choice) and will add pizzazz to any jewelry collection.

Send: $2.00 P&H

Ask For: Fimo Bead Earrings

Mail To: Mostly Art
P.O. Box 24725
Denver, CO 80224-0725

Pets & Animals

THE PURR-FECT TONIC
Catnip Sample

Turn that tiger of a housecat into a frisky kitten with **Mountain Lion catnip**. This minty herb gives cats a natural high, inducing them to roll in it playfully, mew blissfully, frolic, and eventually fall into a peaceful slumber. This safe tonic is grown and harvested by a West Virginia farm family. Each packet contains premium flowers and leaves—no stems—enough for two "helpings."

> **Send:** $1.00 P&H
> **Ask For:** Catnip Sample
> **Mail To:** Mountain Lion
> P.O. Box 120
> Forest Hill, WV 24935-0120

KITTEN CABOODLE
Cat Treats

Keeping Kitty's coat healthy and glossy is a snap with **Cat Snaps,** the irresistible cat treat. Suitable for all cats, these **vitamin and mineral supplements** contain yeast, bonemeal, and dextrine. Each box holds 90 tuna-flavored tablets that will make your pussycat purr with delight.

> **Send:** $2.00 P&H
> **Ask For:** Cat Snaps Treats
> **Mail To:** Prime Pet Products
> P.O. Box 2473
> Beverly Hills, CA 90213
> **Limit:** One per household

NATURE NEWS
Animal Newspaper

For those who love animals, issues regarding their proper treatment are of major concern. Students interested in helping their furry friends will learn all the latest in ***Animal People: News for People Who Care About Animals***. This tabloid-size paper covers a diverse range of subjects, from the use of animals in sacrificial rituals to animal control and rescue to the return of the prairie dog. Send for a **FREE current issue.**

Send: Your name & address

Ask For: Sample copy of *Animal People*

Mail To: Animal People
P.O. Box 960
Clinton, WA 98236-0960

OBJECTING TO DISSECTING
Educational Publications

Each year, many students speak out against **dissection in schools**. What do they know that you don't? Find out in a series of **informative publications** from *Animalearn* magazine. You'll get the scoop on the treatment of animals used in food production, entertainment, and experimentation; dissection and the law; and exercising student rights. Choose from two books: *Vivisection and Dissection in the Classroom* or *Animals in Society,* or select one of five brochures: "What's the Deal with Dissection?" "Dissecting Dissection," "Frog Fact Files," "Dissection and Student Rights," or "The Science Bank: Alternatives to Dissection."

Send: Your name & address ($2.00 P&H for *Animals in Society*)

Ask For: Please specify by title

Mail To: AAVS/Animalearn
801 Old York Rd., #204
Jenkintown, PA 19046-1685

Limit: One per request

Books, Magazines & Newsletters

Computer Software Newsletter

Here's a resource for teachers that provides straight-forward, succinct information on educational software for students ages 2 to 14. Each issue of ***Children's Software,*** a quarterly newsletter, includes an in-depth feature on a particular software genre or topic, such as reference tools, math software, and starting a preschool software library. Regular features include "Preschool Playhouse," which reviews titles for young children, and "The Lookout's Nest," which profiles brand-new software for multiple ages. Send for a **sample issue.**

Send:	$1.00 P&H
Ask For:	Sample issue of *Children's Software*
Mail To:	Children's Software Press
	720 Kuhlman Rd.
	Houston, TX 77024

FDA Reprint

In many ways, the flu is like a cold—both are respiratory infections caused by viruses. How do you avoid these viruses? Learn the facts in **"Colds & Flu,"** a **FREE reprint** from *FDA Consumer* magazine. The reprint explains how to determine whether you have a cold or the flu and reviews over-the-counter medications, flu shots, and home remedies.

Send:	Your name & address
Ask For:	"Colds & Flu"
Mail To:	Food and Drug Administration
	HFI-40
	Rockville, MD 20857

GET METRIC
Metric System Publication

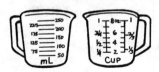

When the United States completes its conversion to the metric system, education and training in math and science will become more efficient and streamlined. From elementary school through graduate school, students will benefit from the transition, creating a "metric-literate" workforce that is better equipped to excel in the global marketplace. Beef up your metric system lesson plans with **"The United States and the Metric System."** Learn about the history of our country's involvement with the metric system, and find the answers to frequently asked questions. Metric conversion charts are also included in this **pamphlet**.

Send: 50¢ P&H
Ask For: "The United States and the Metric System"
Mail To: National Institute of Standards and Technology
Director, Metric Program
Building 820, Room 306
Gaithersburg, MD 20899
Web Site: www.nist.gov/metric

CONSUMER AFFAIRS
Resource Handbook

The Office of Consumer Affairs offers a **FREE** *Consumer's Resource Handbook,* featuring information and advice on how to make the right choices when it comes to automobile purchases or leases, securities investments, consumer assistance resources—just about anything to do with protecting yourself as a consumer.

Send: Your name & address
Ask For: *Consumer's Resource Handbook*
Mail To: U.S. Office of Consumer Affairs
750 17th St. NW
Washington, DC 20006-4607

PRIDE AND JOY
Baby Care Brochure

Newborn babies don't come with instructions—until now. **"The Pediatrician's New Baby Owner's Manual: Your Guide to the Care and Fine-Tuning of Your New Baby"** is filled with straight facts and uncomplicated advice for anxious parents. This **FREE brochure** includes developmental guidelines for baby's first year and tips on how to tell if your child is ill.

Send: LSASE
Ask For: "Baby Owner's Manual" brochure
Mail To: Quill Driver Books
950 Van Ness Ave.
Fresno, CA 93728

THREE STRIKES AND YOU'RE OUT
Anti-Crime Brochure

From Mike Reynolds, author of California's "Three Strikes" initiative, comes a **FREE brochure, "Ten Tips to Help Fight Crime,"** that helps you stop crimes before they can happen. Get advice on becoming an interested and involved voter, reducing your chances of becoming a victim, teaching children to be aware, and arranging for a home security check. The brochure also includes an offer to purchase Reynolds's book, *Three Strikes and You're Out!* at a 30 percent discount.

Send: LSASE
Ask For: "Ten Tips to Help Fight Crime"
Mail To: Quill Driver Books
P.O. Box 4638
Fresno, CA 93744

BEAUCOUP BOOKLETS
Consumer Information Catalog

From student loans to food and nutrition to financial planning, the *Consumer Information Catalog* lists booklets of interest to you and your students that are available at no cost or a nominal fee. Learn safety, home improvement, and travel tips, 66 ways to save money, and how to grow up drug free. Send for a **FREE** copy of the catalog and you may order up to 25 different booklets. The booklets are also available on-line.

Send: Your name & address
Ask For: *Consumer Information Catalog*
Mail To: S. James
CIC-8A
P.O. Box 100
Pueblo, CO 81002
Web Site: www.pueblo.gsa.gov

AISLES OF SAVINGS
Grocery Guide

Learn how to cut your grocery bill in half with *The Grocery Guide* from Tightwad Living. Find out money-saving tips for each department and every aisle of your grocery store, save up to 300 percent on household expenses, and learn how rainchecks can save you big bucks all year long. Want to know how banana peels can save you money? Or how to make day-old bread fresh again? These and other frugal food tips are also featured in this **FREE publication**.

Send: LSASE with two first-class stamps affixed
Ask For: *The Grocery Guide*
Mail To: The Grocery Guide
P.O. Box 629
Burgin, KY 40310-0629
Limit: One per address

IT'S FUN TO REFUND
Publication

Join the parade to savings with **Refundle Bundle**, a bimonthly magazine that lets you discover how fun and rewarding refunding can be. Think rebate and coupon offers aren't worth the trouble? Think again! Each 48-page issue contains $500 worth of current coupon and refund offers, and an explanation of refunding terms. Send for a **sample issue** and start saving today.

Send:	$1.00 P&H
Ask For:	*Refundle Bundle* sample issue
Mail To:	Refundle Bundle
	P.O. Box 140-FB
	Yonkers, NY 10710

THE ROAD TO COLLEGE
Student Loan Booklet

Interested in helping your students or your own child navigate the maze of applying for a student loan? Get your hands on **"All About Direct Loans,"** which describes four types of student education loans, how to apply for a direct loan, what happens while the student is in school, repaying the loan, options for postponing repayment, and what happens if the borrower defaults. Borrower rights and responsibilities, loan consolidation, and entrance counseling are also addressed in this **booklet**.

Send:	$1.00 P&H
Ask For:	"All About Direct Loans" (#505E)
Mail To:	S. James
	CIC-8A
	P.O. Box 100
	Pueblo, CO 81002
Web Site:	www.pueblo.gsa.gov

WOMEN AND SOCIAL SECURITY
Booklet

Almost every American, as a worker or as a dependent of a worker, has Social Security protection. In 1935, when the program was launched, benefits were limited to retired or deceased workers, most of whom were men. Today, with so many women participating in the nation's workforce, the role of women is far different. Whether a woman works, has worked, or has never worked outside the home, she should know exactly what Social Security coverage means to her. Information on benefits on retirement, disability, widowhood, and divorce is covered in a **booklet, "Social Security: What Every Woman Should Know."**

Send: $1.00 P&H

Ask For: "Social Security: What Every Woman Should Know" (#533E)

Mail To: S. James
CIC-8A
P.O. Box 100
Pueblo, CO 81002

Web Site: www.pueblo.gsa.gov

LIFE'S A CIRCUS
Publication

At the beginning of the 20th century, the circus was the most popular form of entertainment, especially for small-town Americans, because it offered spectacles and animals that normally weren't seen in those areas. Teach your students about the circus in America with *Circus Tails*. This publication includes ideas for class activities and a bibliography of circus-related resources.

Send: $1.00 P&H

Ask For: *Circus Tails*

Mail To: Circus World Museum
426 Water St.
Baraboo, WI 53913

WRITING FOR CHILDREN
Pamphlet

For people of any age, writing for children is a great way to exercise the imagination and make a lasting contribution at the same time. A **FREE pamphlet, "How to Get Started as a Children's Writer,"** from *Children's Book Insider* provides indispensable advice for the beginning children's story writer. A step-by-step success plan, an overview of the hottest trends in children's publishing, and the mistakes most commonly made by newcomers are addressed.

> **Send:** LSASE
> **Ask For:** "How to Get Started as a Children's Writer"
> **Mail To:** Report
> Children's Book Insider
> 901 Columbia Rd.
> Fort Collins, CO 80525
> **Web Site:** www.write4kids.com

COUNTING COSTS
Newsletter

Advertisers bombard us with messages to spend, spend, spend, leading many consumers into excessive debt. *Counting the Cost* is a newsletter that encourages you to say no to unnecessary spending and still enjoy more out of life. Learn to practice the art of frugal living through articles on cheap romantic getaways, going from two incomes to one, and cutting costs after having children. With your **FREE sample issue,** you receive a coupon for $2.00 off a one-year subscription.

> **Send:** Your name & address and two loose
> first-class stamps
> **Ask For:** Sample issue
> **Mail To:** Counting the Cost
> 4770 Germantown Rd. Extd., Ste. 122
> Memphis, TN 38141

RX MARKS THE SPOT
FDA Reprint

If you're like most people, you probably have difficulty reading your doctor's handwritten prescriptions. Both the Food and Drug Administration and the American Medical Association are taking steps to remedy this by regulating the information that is included in a prescription. A **FREE reprint** from the FDA lists examples of typical prescriptions and explains terms and symbols to help you decipher that medical "gobbledygook." Send for **"Making It Easier to Read Prescriptions."**

> **Send:** Your name & address
> **Ask For:** "Making It Easier to Read Prescriptions"
> **Mail To:** Food and Drug Administration
> HFI-40
> Rockville, MD 20857

THINGS AREN'T ALWAYS WHAT THEY SEEM
AIM Report

It often doesn't hurt for students to be skeptical while assessing the facts surrounding an issue. Many people believe news reporting by the mainstream media is biased. Get an alternative viewpoint in the *AIM Report*, a **newsletter** published by Accuracy in Media (AIM), the self-proclaimed news media watchdog organization, and help students decide for themselves. You receive the current issue with this offer.

> **Send:** LSASE
> **Ask For:** Free *AIM Report*
> **Mail To:** Accuracy in Media
> 4455 Connecticut Ave., #330
> Washington, DC 20008

TOPS IN SCIENCE
Science Magazine

Science doesn't have to be intimidating for students. In fact, it's one of the most fascinating and interesting school topics. ***TOPS Ideas* science magazine** wants to turn students on to this intriguing field by teaching them about oxidation, magnetism, electricity, probability, and more. Simple, step-by-step experiments and helpful illustrations fill each 16-page publication aimed at promoting hands-on learning in the classroom. Also included are a variety of lesson plans teachers can order.

Send: LSASE

Ask For: Free issue of *TOPS Ideas* teacher offer

Mail To: TOPS Learning Systems
10970 S. Mulino Rd., Dept. FBT
Canby, OR 97013-9747

BE ITALIAN
Italian Club Booklet

From the National Italian American Foundation comes a **FREE booklet** on how to organize an Italian club at your school. What cultural activites to offer, how to write a club constitution, and tips on practical concerns such as balancing the club budget are found in **"How to Successfully Start & Develop an Italian Club at Your School."**

Send: Your name & address

Ask For: Italian Club Book

Mail To: The National Italian American Foundation
1860 19th St. NW
Washington, DC 20009-5501

YO-YO MANIA
Newsletter

The sport of the yo-yo has its—ahem—ups and downs, but no matter what age you are or what grade you're in, if you're a true student of the yo-yo, then the **Yo-Yo Times** is for you. Your **sample issue** of this newsletter contains articles and information on the culture of yo in addition to new tricks, tips, ideas, upcoming contests, contest results, and classified ads.

Send: $1.00 P&H
Ask For: *Yo-Yo Times* sample issue
Mail To: Yo-Yo Times newsletter
P.O. Box 1519-FB
Herndon, VA 20172

DON'T WAIT . . . CONSOLIDATE!
Student Loan Information

Are student loans driving you crazy? Consolidating your federal loans into a single account could benefit you financially. You can pay based on your income, give yourself more repayment choices, and change your repayment plan at any time. It's all in a **booklet** called **"Consolidate with Direct Loans."** Also included are criteria to help you decide if consolidation is right for you, and sample payment charts for various incomes.

Send: $1.00 P&H
Ask For: "Consolidate with Direct Loans"
Mail To: S. James
CIC-8A
P.O. Box 100
Pueblo, CO 81002
Web Site: www.pueblo.gsa.gov

YOUR FINANCIAL FUTURE
Investment Information

Have you invested your earnings wisely? Would you like guidance in setting up a college fund for your children? Are you interested in finding out effective ways to help your money grow? Get the facts you need to make wise investment decisions with **FREE information** from the U.S. Securities and Exchange Commission. Write for a listing of available information.

Send: Your name & address
Ask For: Investment information
Mail To: U.S. Securities and Exchange Commission
Office of Publications
Washington, DC 20549

THE RETIRING TYPE
IRA Information

If you are making plans to retire, or if you have already retired, you need help finding your way through the mazes that surround Social Security, distribution of pension/retirement plans, retirement planning, and other financial topics. The Internal Revenue Service requires you to take a minimum required distribution (MRD) from your Individual Retirement Accounts by the time you reach age 70¼. In addition, you must pick one of two withdrawal methods: recalculation or declining balance. Fidelity Investments offers a **FREE brochure, "Taking Your MRD."**

Phone: 1-800-544-5373
Ask For: "Taking Your MRD"

GROWING PAINS

Pamphlets

Illustrated with the popular characters from the comic strip "Peanuts," these **FREE pamphlets** from MetLife are fun and informative. Contact MetLife and ask for any of the pamphlets listed below.

Phone: 1-800-MET-LIFE (638-5433)
Web Site: www.metlife.com

"Your Child's First Day at School" gives advice on coaching your child on how to participate, cooperate, and communicate on an exciting yet stressful day, and helps you determine if both of you are ready for the big day.

Ask For: "Your Child's First Day at School" (#505)

"Protecting Your Child" provides tips on teaching safety rules, what to do if you believe a child is missing, and strategies for promoting good communication.

Ask For: "Protecting Your Child" (#507)

"Helping Your Child Understand Money" covers goal setting, savings accounts, setting up a personal budget, and privacy issues.

Ask For: "Helping Your Child Understand Money" (#501)

"Your Child and Organized Sports" gives advice on encouraging a healthy, active lifestyle in your child, getting a doctor's OK, and teaching the concept of fair play.

Ask For: "Your Child and Organized Sports" (#511)

Travel

TO YOUR HEALTH
Information for Travelers

"Don't drink the water" is good advice, but in certain parts of the world, where other health hazards are present, vaccinations may be needed prior to travel. Call the Centers for Disease Control's (CDC) toll-free number to receive information by fax on health risks and recent disease outbreaks in specific geographic areas. More than 60 different **health faxes** are available.

Phone: 1-888-232-3299
1-888-232-3228 if you don't have a fax
Ask For: Please specify by topic
Web Site: www.cdc.gov (highlight "Travelers' Health")

GIVE ME A BRAKE
Safety Brochure

If your automobile is equipped with an anti-lock braking system (ABS)—and more than half of all new cars sold in North America are—you should have this informative **brochure** from the ABS Education Alliance. **"America Brakes for Safety"** explains how the mechanism works and how to determine when your car's ABS is working. Also covered are tips for driving with ABS and a list of dos and don'ts of proper ABS usage.

Send: LSASE
Ask For: ABS Education Alliance brochure
Mail To: ABS Education Alliance
P.O. Box 13966
Research Triangle Park, NC 27709-3966
Web Site: www.abs-education.org

Travel Brochures

Being prepared and staying safe are keys to successful travel. Budgetel Inns offers two **FREE brochures. "Tips for Today's Business Traveler"** tells you what to pack and how to pack it right, how to juggle your time effectively in the air and on the road, and what safety features to look for when choosing accommodations. **"Tips for Today's Woman Traveler"** focuses on how to evaluate the level of hotel security, plan ahead, and be a confident traveler.

> **Phone:** 1-800-4-BUDGET (428-3438)
> **Ask For:** "Tips for Today's Business Traveler" or "Tips for Today's Woman Traveler"

RV Tire Care Guide

Whether you favor weekend trips or yearlong odysseys in your recreational vehicle, this **RV tire care and safety guide** is one you shouldn't be without. Learn about proper tire inflation, how to weigh your RV or travel trailer, the dangers of overloading your vehicle and using the wrong size tire, and tips on making repairs in this helpful 22-page booklet. Happy trails!

> **Send:** LSASE
> **Ask For:** RV Tire Care & Safety Guide
> **Mail To:** Tire Industry Safety Council
> P.O. Box 3147
> Medina, OH 44258
> **Web Site:** www.TISC.org

TENDER LOVING CAR CARE
Brochures

Do you know what to do in a roadside emergency? What signs tell you that your car needs a tune-up? Why is a drive train important? The Car Care Council wants you to stay safe by practicing regular maintenance and repairs on your vehicle. Choose from 11 **car maintenance brochures:**

"A Roadside Emergency: Would You Know What to Do?"

"An Annual Physical for My Car?"

"How to Find Your Way Under the Hood & Around the Car"

"Winter . . . Are You and Your Car Ready?"

"The Eight Most Common Signs Your Car Needs a Tune-Up"

"What You Should Know About Your Car's Drive Train"

"How to Keep Your Wheels on the Road"

"How to Help Your Car Keep Its Cool"

"Keep an Eye on Your Car's Filters"

"How to Keep Your Brakes from Letting You Down"

"Which Way to Go? Replace or Rebuild"

Send: LSASE

Ask For: Please specify by title

Mail To: Car Care Council
Dept. FB8
42 Park Drive
Port Clinton, OH 43452

KEEPING KIDS SAFE
Family Travel Tips

Family trips bring people closer together and create a wealth of happy memories. To make your trip as safe and fun as possible, it's important to stay alert. A **FREE information leaflet** from Budgetel Inns describes important precautions and offers the following tips for "KidSafe" travel: choose a safe place to stay, review and role-play standard safety rules, practice the buddy system, and carry identification for each child.

Phone: 1-800-4-BUDGET (428-3438)
Ask For: "KidSafe Traveler"

IN THE DRIVER'S SEAT
Teacher's Information Packet

With this **car care information packet** from Armor All, you can help student drivers learn how to keep a car running smoothly and looking like new through simple maintenance procedures. Designed for both high school and driving school instructors, this **FREE** packet includes a video, teacher's guide, student handouts and quizzes, car care brochures, and samples of Armor All protectant.

Send: Your name, class taught, school, and address
Ask For: "Armor All Guide to Total Car Care"
Mail To: P.O. Box 26629
San Francisco, CA 94126-6629

OFF THE BEATEN PATH
Travel Newsletter

Want to visit a lunar landscape on Earth? See where Coca-Cola was originally bottled? Dig for diamonds in the United States? See the world's largest catsup bottle? Get your hands on a **sample issue** of *Yesterday's Highways,* a newsletter devoted to oddities found off the interstate. Explore small towns, offbeat museums, and roads and trails where American history was made. Road trips will never be the same!

Send: $1.00 P&H
Ask For: *Yesterday's Highways* Sample
Mail To: Yesterday's Highways Newsletter
49 Church St., Ste. F
Weaverville, NC 28787-9420

CHEAP STAYS
Hostel Handbook

For students, backpackers, and budget travelers alike, hostels are a welcome type of lodging—they're convenient, clean, and easy on the wallet. More than 600 budget accommodations in the United States and Canada are listed in the **Hostel Handbook,** updated every spring. The handbook also gives information on inexpensive ground transportation, driving cross-country, and bus, airline, and train service. The booklet fits easily into a backpack or back pocket.

Send: $2.00 P&H
Ask For: The Hostel Handbook
Mail To: Hostel Handbook
44 Andover St.
Ludlow, VT 05149

TIRED AND TRUE
Tire Care Brochure

People spend a large portion of their lives behind the wheel of a car. For your safety as well as that of your passengers, make sure that when you head out on the highway, your car's tires are properly maintained and cared for. The Tire Industry Safety Council's **brochure on tire care** tells you how to inspect tires and decide which tire is right for your car or light truck. Good driving habits, inflation tips, proper storage, and tire rotation patterns are also found in this fact-filled brochure.

Send:	LSASE
Ask For:	Tire Care Brochure
Mail To:	Tire Industry Safety Council
	P.O. Box 3147
	Medina, OH 44258
Web Site:	www.TISC.org

HOSTEL TERRITORY
Hostelling Map

Hostels offer low-cost, dormitory-style lodging and are an inexpensive way to enjoy whatever area you visit. The nonprofit group Hostelling International–American Youth Hostels (HI-AYH) publishes a **FREE "Hostelling Map of the USA."** Updated yearly, the map has locations and addresses of more than 125 hostels across the country. The hostels are open to all travelers, but rates are cheaper if you are an HI-AYH member.

Phone:	202-783-6161
	or
Send:	Your name & address
Ask For:	"Hostelling Map of the USA"
Mail To:	HI-AYH
	733 15th St. NW, #840
	Washington, DC 20005

ON A SHOESTRING
Budget Hotel Directory

Planning your next vacation? Don't leave home without a copy of the **Budget Host Travel Directory**. This **FREE guide** is bursting with information on the Budget Host network of more than 170 affiliated, mostly family-owned economy inns throughout the United States and Canada. AAA and Mobil Travel Guide ratings are provided, along with maps and descriptions of each inn's or motel's amenities.

Phone: 1-800-BUD-HOST (283-4678)
Ask For: "Budget Host Travel Directory"
Web Site: www.budgethost.com

BEATING THE USED-CAR HUSTLE
Auto Hotline

Buying a used car saves money, but in order to avoid getting ripped off, you need to do your homework beforehand. Before you buy a used car, check newspaper ads to determine a fair price. Once you know what type of car you want, you can obtain **recall information** on that vehicle for **FREE**. Authorized dealers of that make and model are obligated, by law, to do recall work for FREE, no matter how old the car. Call the Auto Safety Hotline for more information.

Phone: 1-800-424-9393

LEARNING ABOUT LEMON LAWS
Booklet

Almost all states have "lemon laws," which enable an owner to get a refund or replacement when a new vehicle turns out to have a substantial problem that is not fixed within a reasonable number of attempts. If you suspect your new car is a "lemon," send for this **FREE booklet, "Lemon Law Summary,"** to learn more.

Send: LSASE with two first-class stamps affixed
Ask For: "Lemon Law Summary"
Mail To: Center for Auto Safety
2001 S St. NW, #410
Washington, DC 20009

DISCOVER AMERICA
Tourism Offices Guide

It's a big country out there, and before you and your family take off on your next road trip, you want to know where you're going and what to see. **"Discover America"** lists tourism offices throughout the United States. Use this list to order **FREE** maps, calendars of events, and travel guides containing information on accommodations, campgrounds, points of interest, restaurants, attractions, recreation activities, and more.

Send: $1.00 P&H
Ask For: "Discover America: A Listing of State Tourism Offices of the U.S." (#363E)
Mail To: S. James
CIC-8A
P.O. Box 100
Pueblo, CO 81002
Web Site: www.pueblo.gsa.gov

On the Internet

As every teacher knows, computers are an important part of the classroom. Teachers have discovered that computer programs and Internet Web sites not only can serve as great informational resources, but they also bring variation and inspiration into the classroom by encouraging students to investigate areas of interest to them and to solve problems on their own.

The editors at *FREEBIES* understand that navigating the information superhighway is not always easy. This section focuses on sites on the World Wide Web that are user-friendly, educational, and fun to explore.

INTERNET SAFETY
Brochure

The vast amount of information and educational material on the Internet makes it a wonderful resource for students. Both teachers and parents, however, have serious concerns regarding the dangers of the "great on-line abyss." A **brochure** called **"Safety First: Children and the Internet"** helps teachers guide students in responsible use of the Internet. Featured are suggestions for specific age groups, guidelines for parental control, tips on dealing with E-mail problems, and a list of Web sites for children and teachers.

Send: $1.00 P&H

Ask For: Internet Safety Brochure

Mail To: Children's Software Press
720 Kuhlman Rd.
Houston, TX 77024

MONEY MATTERS
Debt Management Advice

Would you pay $96 for a bill that totals $20? That's what many people who are in credit card debt are doing without even knowing it. Scott Bilker, whose money-saving advice has been featured on TV, radio, and in magazines, is the author of ***Credit Card and Debt Management: A Step-by-Step Guide for Organizing Debts and Saving Money on Interest Payments.*** Download one chapter from this valuable book on the Internet.

Web Address: http://www.debtsmart.com/freebies.html

FOR A CLEAN ENVIRONMENT
Tree-Planting Project

If the simple act of planting a tree inspires others to do the same, the environment would benefit greatly. Log on to the **Kids FACE** (Kids For A Clean Environment) Web site and download the steps involved to create a fun **tree-planting project** for your students. You learn how to select a planting site, how to acquire a tree, and proper procedures for planting the tree, plus tips on tree care, including how to make a "mulch blanket." Kids FACE is headed by two young girls who have continued to develop and implement community programs locally, nationally, and worldwide to improve the environment.

Web Address: http://www.kidsface.org

ONE SWEET SITE
Educational Web Site

Inspired by the classic children's book *Charlie and the Chocolate Factory,* the **Willy Wonka Candy Factory® Web site** is a fun, educational site targeted at ages 6 to 11. Students navigate through Willy's factory on the Wonkavator, accessing various rooms along the way. Each room has its own theme, such as astronomy, technology, animals, and science, and features games, activities, trivia, and downloadable items for use in the classroom. The site's teacher section has ready-to-use lesson plans on math, science, and other subjects.

Web Address: http://www.wonka.com

UNDERSTANDING SOCIAL SECURITY
SSA Information

Learn about the benefits and services provided by the **Social Security Administration** (SSA) by logging on to the SSA's official Web site. A special children's page called **Youthlink** explains what every kid, teen, parent, and teacher should know about Social Security. The site also disseminates disability information, how to apply for services, employment opportunities, and information on SSA business services, budget and planning, and reporting fraud.

Web Address: http://www.ssa.gov

WHAT'S YOUR TYPE?
Money Personality Questionnaire

When it comes to money, are you a risk taker or are you more conservative? Should you invest in small cap stocks or blue chips? A questionnaire is available on the Mutual Fund Alliance Web site to help find the answers to these questions. Developed by Dr. Kathleen Gurney, an expert in the psychology of investing, **"The Moneymax Profile"** gives you insight into your money personality. The profile takes about 10 minutes to complete and helps you identify which of nine major money types fits your profile.

Web Address: http://www.mfea.com/

OPEN UP
Internet Guidance

Project OPEN is a joint effort of the National Consumers League and the Interactive Services Association. Its primary mission is to help consumers understand how to use on-line and Internet services. Their **FREE brochure, "How to Get the Most Out of Going On-line,"** describes tools to help educators and parents screen on-line content for students and children.

Phone: 1-800-466-OPEN (466-6736)
Ask For: "How to Get the Most Out of Going On-line"

TAKING STOCK
Stock Exchange Information

In 1792, a group of 20 stockbrokers met in New York City to determine market rates on stocks-and-bonds commissions. From this agreement, the New York Stock Exchange was born. If New York City is too far for you to visit, drop in on the New York or NASDAQ **stock exchanges** via your computer.

Web Addresses: http://www.nyse.com
http://www.nasdaq.com

THE BEST YEARS OF YOUR LIFE
Retirement Planning Information

Your retirement is to be savored and enjoyed. It should be your reward for years of hard work, and you deserve to feel financially secure as you enter your golden years.

The International Society of Retirement Planning has a Web site that provides helpful **information and advice** on planning your retirement.

Web Address: http://www.isrplan.org

To increase your financial IQ and further develop your **investment and growth strategy** visit the following Web site.

Web Address: http://www.investorprotection.org

Review your current **retirement savings plan** to determine if there will be enough funds for your eventual retirement lifestyle plan using the Web site below. Once you enter the Web site, click on "Retirement" under tools.

Web Address: http://www.Pathfinder.com/money

DESTINATION UNKNOWN?
Travel Sites

You've got some vacation time coming up, but where to go? Hop on to the Internet and uncover a treasure trove of **destination ideas** with these informative Web pages:

> www.frommers.com
> www.fodors.com
> www.lonelyplanet.com

Once you know where you want to go, visit these sites to find **budget travel accommodations:**

> www.budgettravel.com/specials.htm
> www.stratpub.com
> www.savtraveler.com

Many of us know where we want to go when we hit the road on vacation, but we often need help getting there. **Directions** to almost anywhere in the United States—including where to turn and even mileage between turns—can be found by steering to the following Web site:

> www.mapsonus.com

Learn more about traveling to foreign destinations by connecting to **embassy sites** worldwide via the Internet.

> www.embpage.org

Then check out the following Web site to learn basic phrases in 25 **languages**.

> www.travlang.com/languages

Another top family-friendly site is the **Family Travel Forum**. Here you can post questions and comments to other parents and find links to family-oriented travel agencies.

> www.familytravelforum.com

SPORTS ON-LINE

Team Information

For you "cybersport fan-atics" who just can't get enough of your favorite sports team, below is a list of several sites to check out. This is the fastest way to send fan mail or get up-to-date information on all your favorite athletes.

Basketball Hall of Fame
http://www.hooptown.com/

College football
http://cbs.sportsline.com/u/football/college/index.html

Continental Basketball Association
http://www.cbahoops.com

Major League Baseball
http://www.majorleaguebaseball.com

Major League Soccer
http://www.mlsnet.com/

National Basketball Association
http://www.nba.com

National Collegiate Athletic Association
http://www.ncaa.org/champs/baseball/

National Football League
http://www.nfl.com

National Hockey League
http://www.nhl.com/

National Wheelchair Basketball Association
http://www.nwba.org

Women's National Basketball Association
http://www.wnba.com

Sports

SHAD SOME LIGHT ON THE MATTER
Fishing Bait

How do you reel in crappie, perch, and bream? The secret is in the shad—the **Cajun Shad,** that is. This artificial bait can be used with an old cane pole or ultralight tackle. A weight is already molded into the head of the lure, so no pinch-on weight is needed. The Cajun Shad can be used with or without a cork.

Send: $1.00 P&H for one; $2.00 for three
Ask For: Cajun Shad
Mail To: Ol' John's Lures
7979 Hwy. 3015
Keatchie, LA 71046

IN THE BIG LEAGUES
Publication, Bumper Sticker, and Player Card

Sports fans know that senior circuit stars such as Anthony Mason, Spud Webb, and Mario Elie got their start in the United States Basketball League (USBL). Since its inception in 1984, the USBL has served as the proving ground for hoopsters who were talented yet not quite ready for the NBA. Send for a copy of the **USBL *Leaguewide Publication*** and you also receive a team **bumper sticker** and collectible **player card** (supplier's choice).

Send: $2.00 P&H
Ask For: USBL Publication, Sticker, and Card
Mail To: USBL
46 Quirk Rd.
Milford, CT 06460

SAFETY ON WHEELS
In-line Skating Safety Program

At the beach, on the sidewalks, and in rinks around the country, in-line skating is increasing in popularity, and so is the number of skating-related injuries. Safe skating has become an issue concerning children, teens, parents, teachers, and anyone who has ever encountered an inexperienced skater. The Roller Skating Association's (RSA) **skating safety program** contains skating guidelines and tips, a poster, a safe skating certificate for students who pass a skills test, and a set of five stickers featuring the RSA's mascot, Roller Roo.

Send: $2.00 P&H
Ask For: In-line Skating Safety Tips Program
Mail To: Roller Skating Association
6905 Corporate Drive
Indianapolis, IN 46278
Attn: Accounting
Web Site: www.rollerskating.org

TOUCHDOWN RECEPTION
Football Fan Packages

Here's the play: Students huddle at their desks and write a letter requesting a **FREE NFL Fan Pack** from their favorite professional football team. They mail it to the address below, and in a few weeks they'll score with a cool package of NFL stuff geared toward young fans. The fan package may include an NFL calendar, newsletter, trading cards, and other terrific offers (contents of the package may vary). High-step into the end zone and score your order today.

Send: Your name & address
Ask For: NFL Fan pack (please specify team)
Mail To: Starline Sports Marketing
Freebies Offer
1480 Terrell Mill Rd.
P.O. Box 700
Marietta, GA 30067

FAN-TASTIC FREEBIES
Fan Packages

Most professional sports franchises have **FREE materials,** such as season schedules and ticket information, that they give away to enthusiastic fans. Some teams even offer free fan packages that may contain stickers, photos, catalogs, fan club information, and more. These souvenirs can be a great reward for hardworking students and make colorful additions to the classroom.

To get these items, all you need to do is write to your students' favorite team from the following list. Include your name and address and ask for a "fan package." Although not all teams require it, you should send an LSASE to help speed your request. Be sure to include extra postage when writing to Canada. The post office can tell you the current rates for Canada.

If you want to contact a specific player on a team, address the envelope to his or her attention. Keep in mind that because of the high volume of fan mail each team receives, it may take at least eight weeks or more to get a response.

Web site addresses are also listed for some teams. To get more information on your teams through the Internet, see page 111. Many sports organizations provide links to their teams.

AMERICAN LEAGUE BASEBALL TEAMS

Anaheim Angels
P.O. Box 2000
Anaheim, CA 92803

Baltimore Orioles
333 W. Camden St.
Baltimore, MD 21201

Boston Red Sox
Fenway Park
Boston, MA 02215

Chicago White Sox
333 W. 35th St.
Chicago, IL 60616

Cleveland Indians
2401 Ontario St.
Cleveland, OH 44115

Detroit Tigers
2121 Trumbull Ave.
Detroit, MI 48216

Kansas City Royals
P.O. Box 419969
Kansas City, MO 64141

Minnesota Twins
34 Kirby Puckett Place
Minneapolis, MN 55415

New York Yankees
Yankee Stadium
Bronx, NY 10451

Oakland Athletics
7677 Oakport, Ste. 200
Oakland, CA 94621

Seattle Mariners
P.O. Box 4100
Seattle, WA 98104

Tampa Bay Devil Rays
One Tropicana Drive
St. Petersburg, FL 33705

Texas Rangers
P.O. Box 90111
Arlington, TX 76004

Toronto Blue Jays
One Blue Jays Way,
Ste. 3200
Toronto, Ontario
Canada M5V 1J1
(Note: First-class mail to Canada requires extra stamps.)

NATIONAL LEAGUE BASEBALL TEAMS

Arizona Diamondbacks
P.O. Box 2095
Phoenix, AZ 85001

Atlanta Braves
P.O. Box 4064
Atlanta, GA 30303

Chicago Cubs
1060 W. Addison St.
Chicago, IL 60613-4397

Cincinnati Reds
100 Cinergy Field
Cincinnati, OH 45202

Colorado Rockies
2001 Blake St.
Denver, CO 80205

Florida Marlins
2267 NW 199th St.
Miami, FL 33056

Houston Astros
P.O. Box 288
Houston, TX 77001

Los Angeles Dodgers
1000 Elysian Park Ave.
Los Angeles, CA 90012-1199

Milwaukee Brewers
Milwaukee County Stadium
P.O. Box 3099
Milwaukee, WI 53201-3099

Montreal Expos
P.O. Box 500, Station M
Montreal, Quebec
Canada H1V 3P2
(Note: First-class mail to Canada requires extra stamps.)

New York Mets
Shea Stadium
Flushing, NY 11368

Philadelphia Phillies
P.O. Box 7575
Philadelphia, PA 19101

Pittsburgh Pirates
P.O. Box 7000
Pittsburgh, PA 15212

St. Louis Cardinals
250 Stadium Plaza
St. Louis, MO 63102

San Diego Padres
P.O. Box 2000
San Diego, CA 92112-2000

San Francisco Giants
3Com Park at Candlestick Point
San Francisco, CA 94124

NATIONAL BASKETBALL ASSOCIATION TEAMS

Atlanta Hawks
One CNN Center
South Tower, Ste. 405
Atlanta, GA 30303

Boston Celtics
151 Merrimac St., 5th Floor
Boston, MA 02114

Charlotte Hornets
100 Hive Drive
Charlotte, NC 28217

Chicago Bulls
United Center
1901 W. Madison St.
Chicago, IL 60612

Cleveland Cavaliers
Gund Arena
One Center Court
Cleveland, OH 44115

Dallas Mavericks
Reunion Arena
777 Sports St.
Dallas, TX 75207

Denver Nuggets
1635 Clay St.
P.O. Box 4658
Denver, CO 80204-0658

Detroit Pistons
The Palace of Auburn Hills
Two Championship Drive
Auburn Hills, MI 48326

Golden State Warriors
1011 Broadway, 20th Floor
Oakland, CA 94607

Houston Rockets
Two Greenway Plaza, Ste. 400
Houston, TX 77046

Indiana Pacers
300 E. Market St.
Indianapolis, IN 46204

Los Angeles Clippers
L.A. Sports Arena
3939 S. Figueroa St.
Los Angeles, CA 90037

Los Angeles Lakers
The Great Western Forum
3900 W. Manchester Blvd.
Inglewood, CA 90306

Miami Heat
Miami Arena
SunTrust International
Center
One SE Third Ave.,
Ste. 2300
Miami, FL 33131

Milwaukee Bucks
The Bradley Center
1001 N. Fourth St.
Milwaukee, WI 53203-1312

Minnesota Timberwolves
Target Center
600 First Ave. N.
Minneapolis, MN 55403

New Jersey Nets
405 Murray Hill Pkwy.
East Rutherford, NJ 07073

New York Knickerbockers
Madison Square Garden
Two Pennsylvania Plaza
New York, NY 10121

Orlando Magic
RDV Sportsplex
Two Magic Place
8701 Maitland Summit Blvd.
Orlando, FL 32810

Philadelphia 76ers
One CoreStates Complex
Philadelphia, PA 19148

Phoenix Suns
America West Arena
201 E. Jefferson
Phoenix, AZ 85004

Portland Trail Blazers
One Center Court, Ste. 200
Portland, OR 97227

Sacramento Kings
One Sports Pkwy.
Sacramento, CA 95834

San Antonio Spurs
100 Montana St.
San Antonio, TX 78203

Seattle Supersonics
490 5th Ave. N.
Seattle, WA 98109

Toronto Raptors
20 Bay St., Ste. 1702
Toronto, Ontario
Canada MSJ 2N8
*(Note: First-class mail to
Canada requires extra
stamps.)*

Utah Jazz
Delta Center
301 W. South Temple
Salt Lake City, UT 84101

Vancouver Grizzlies
General Motors Place
800 Griffiths Way
Vancouver, British
Columbia
Canada V6B 6G1
*(Note: First-class mail to
Canada requires extra
stamps.)*

Washington Wizards
MCI Center
601 F St. NW
Washington, DC 20001

WOMEN'S NATIONAL BASKETBALL ASSOCIATION TEAMS

Charlotte Sting
3308 Oak Lake Blvd., Ste. B
Charlotte, NC 28208

Cleveland Rockers
One Center Court
Cleveland, OH 44115

Detroit Shock
Two Championship Drive
Auburn Hills, MI 48326

Houston Comets
Two Greenway Plaza,
Ste. 400
Houston, TX 77046-3865

Los Angeles Sparks
P.O. Box 10
Inglewood, CA 90306

Minnesota (TBD)
600 1st Ave. N.
Minneapolis, MN 55403

New York Liberty
Two Pennsylvania Plaza
New York, NY 10121

Orlando (TBD)
RDV Sportsplex
8701 Maitland Summit Blvd.
Orlando, FL 32801

Phoenix Mercury
201 E. Jefferson St.
Phoenix, AZ 85004

Sacramento Monarchs
One Sports Pkwy.
Sacramento, CA 95834

Utah Starzz
301 W. South Temple
Salt Lake City, UT 84101

Washington Mystics
601 F St., NW
Washington, DC 20001

AMERICAN FOOTBALL CONFERENCE TEAMS

Baltimore Ravens
11001 Owings Mills Rd.
Owings Mills, MD 21117

Buffalo Bills
One Bills Drive
Orchard Park, NY 14127

Cincinnati Bengals
One Bengals Drive
Cincinnati, OH 45204

Cleveland Browns Trust
80 First Ave.
Berea, OH 44017

Denver Broncos
13655 Broncos Pkwy.
Englewood, CO 80112

Indianapolis Colts
7001 W. 56th St.
Indianapolis, IN 46254

Jacksonville Jaguars
One ALLTEL Stadium Place
Jacksonville, FL 32202

Kansas City Chiefs
One Arrowhead Drive
Kansas City, MO 64129

Miami Dolphins
7500 SW 30th St.
Davie, FL 33329

New England Patriots
Foxboro Stadium/Rte. 1
Foxboro, MA 02035

New York Jets
1000 Fulton Ave.
Hempstead, NY 11550

Oakland Raiders
1220 Harbor Bay Pkwy.
Alameda, CA 94502

Pittsburgh Steelers
300 Stadium Circle
Pittsburgh, PA 15212

San Diego Chargers
Qualcomm Stadium
San Diego, CA 92123

Seattle Seahawks
11220 NE 53rd St.
Kirkland, WA 98033

Tennessee Oilers
Baptist Sports Park
7640 Hwy. 70 S.
Nashville, TN 37221

NATIONAL FOOTBALL CONFERENCE TEAMS

Arizona Cardinals
8701 S. Hardy Drive
Phoenix, AZ 85284-2800

Atlanta Falcons
One Falcon Place
Suwanee, GA 30174

Carolina Panthers
800 S. Mint St.
Charlotte, NC 28202

Chicago Bears
1000 Football Drive
Lake Forest, IL 60045

Dallas Cowboys
One Cowboys Pkwy.
Irving, TX 75063

Detroit Lions
1200 Featherstone Rd.
Pontiac, MI 48342

Green Bay Packers
1265 Lombardi Ave.
Green Bay, WI 54307

Minnesota Vikings
9520 Viking Drive
Eden Prairie, MN 55344

New Orleans Saints
5800 Airline Hwy.
Metairie, LA 70003

New York Giants
Giants Stadium
East Rutherford, NJ 07073

Philadelphia Eagles
3501 S. Broad St.
Philadelphia, PA 19148

St. Louis Rams
One Rams Way
St. Louis, MO 63045

San Francisco 49ers
4949 Centennial Blvd.
Santa Clara, CA 95054

Tampa Bay Buccaneers
One Buccaneer Place
Tampa, FL 33607

Washington Redskins
21300 Redskin Park Drive
Ashburn, VA 20147

NATIONAL HOCKEY LEAGUE TEAMS

Atlanta Thrashers
One CNN Center
12th S. Tower
Atlanta, GA 30303

Boston Bruins
Fleet Center
Boston, MA 02114

Buffalo Sabres
Marine Midland Arena
One Seymour H. Knox III
Plaza
Buffalo, NY 14203-3096

Calgary Flames
Canadian Airlines
Saddledome
Box 1540—Station M
Calgary, Alberta
Canada T2P 3B9
*(Note: First-class mail to
Canada requires extra
stamps.)*

Carolina Hurricanes
5000 Aerial Ctr., Ste. 100
Morrisville, NC 27560

Chicago Blackhawks
1901 W. Madison St.
Chicago, IL 60612

Colorado Avalanche
McNichols Sports Arena
1635 Clay St.
Denver, CO 80204-1799

Columbus Blue Jackets
150 E. Wilson Bridge Rd.,
Ste. 235
Worthington, OH 43085

Dallas Stars
Dr. Pepper StarCenter
211 Cowboys Pkwy.
Irving, TX 75063

Detroit Red Wings
Joe Louis Arena
600 Civic Center Drive
Detroit, MI 48226

Edmonton Oilers
11230-110 St.
Edmonton, Alberta
Canada T5G 3G8
*(Note: First-class mail to
Canada requires extra
stamps.)*

Florida Panthers
National Car Rental Center
One Panthers Parkway
Sunrise, FL 33323

Los Angeles Kings
The Great Western Forum
3900 W. Manchester Blvd.
Inglewood, CA 90305

Mighty Ducks of Anaheim
Arrowhead Pond of
Anaheim
2695 Katella Ave.
Anaheim, CA 92803

Minnesota Wild
444 Cedar St., Ste. 900
St. Paul, MN 55101

Montreal Canadiens
1260 rue de la Gauchetiere
Ouest
Montreal, Quebec
Canada H3B 5E8
*(Note: First-class mail to
Canada requires extra stamps.)*

Nashville Predators
501 Broadway
Nashville, TN 37203

New Jersey Devils
Continental Airlines Arena
50 Rte. 120 N.
East Rutherford, NJ 07073

New York Islanders
Nassau Coliseum
Uniondale, NY 11553

New York Rangers
Madison Square Garden
Two Pennsylvania Plaza,
14th Floor
New York, NY 10121

Ottawa Senators
Corel Centre
1000 Palladium Drive
Kanata, Ontario
Canada K2V 1A5
*(Note: First-class mail to
Canada requires extra stamps.)*

Philadelphia Flyers
First Union Center
3601 S. Broad St.
Philadelphia, PA 19148

Phoenix Coyotes
Cellular One Den
9375 E. Bell Rd.
Scottsdale, AZ 85260

Pittsburgh Penguins
Civic Arena
66 Mario Lemieux Place
Pittsburgh, PA 15219

St. Louis Blues
1401 Clark Ave.
St. Louis, MO 63103

San Jose Sharks
San Jose Arena
525 W. Santa Clara St.
San Jose, CA 95113

Tampa Bay Lightning
Ice Palace
401 Channelside Drive
Tampa, FL 33602

Toronto Maple Leafs
Maple Leaf Gardens
60 Carlton St.
Toronto, Ontario
Canada M5B 1L1
*(Note: First-class mail to
Canada requires extra stamps.)*

Vancouver Canucks
General Motors Place
800 Griffiths Way
Vancouver, British
Columbia
Canada V6B 6G1
*(Note: First-class mail to
Canada requires extra stamps.)*

Washington Capitals
601 F St., NW
Washington, DC 20004

MAJOR LEAGUE SOCCER—WESTERN CONFERENCE

Chicago Fire
311 W. Superior St., #444
Chicago, IL 60610

Colorado Rapids
555 17th St., Ste. 3350
Denver, CO 80202

Dallas Burn
2602 McKinney, Ste. 200
Dallas, TX 75204

Kansas City Wizards
706 Broadway St., Ste. 100
Kansas City, MO 64105-2300

L.A. Galaxy
1640 S. Sepulveda Blvd.,
Ste. 114
Los Angeles, CA 90025

San Jose Clash
1265 El Camino Real,
2nd Floor
Santa Clara, CA 95050

MAJOR LEAGUE SOCCER—EASTERN CONFERENCE

Columbus Crew
77 E. Nationwide Blvd.
Columbus, OH 43215

D.C. United
13832 Redskin Dr.
Herndon, VA 22071

Metrostars
One Harmon Plaza,
8th Floor
Secaucus, NJ 07094

Miami Fusion
2200 Commercial Blvd.,
Ste. 104
Ft. Lauderdale, Fl. 33309

New England Revolution
Foxboro Stadium, Rte. 1
Foxboro, MA 02035

Tampa Bay Mutiny
1408 N. Westshore Blvd.,
Ste. 1004
Tampa, FL 33607

Odds & Ends

Mini Sewing Kit

Wherever you go, you never know when you might lose a button or need a safety pin to secure a wayward strap or other clothing item. With this **mini travel sewing kit,** you have everything you need for those little jobs: an assortment of different-colored threads, scissors, safety pins, and a tape measure, all neatly packed in a tiny coin-purse-size container.

> **Send:** LSASE plus $2.00 P&H
> **Ask For:** Mini Travel Sewing Kit
> **Mail To:** The Complete Collegiate
> 490 Rte. 46 East
> Fairfield, NJ 07704

Hug Coupons

When you see a friend or family member feeling down, or if you're feeling blue yourself, pull out one of these **FREE hug coupons** and turn that frown upside down. You also receive a sample issue of the *Let's Hug* newsletter along with your business card–size hug coupons. The coupons are great for birthdays, Valentine's Day, anniversaries, or just anytime someone is in need of a big hug.

> **Send:** LSASE
> **Ask For:** *Let's Hug* newsletter and hug coupons
> **Mail To:** Let's Hug—F99
> P.O. Box 2178
> Port Washington, NY 11050
> **Limit:** One per household

DORM ESSENTIALS
Catalog and Checklist

For most college-bound students moving into a dormitory, it's their first time away from home, a time of both excitement and anxiety. A **FREE catalog** of necessities and gifts for the college-bound also serves as a convenient dorm **checklist**. From lamps to calculators, pencil sharpeners to clothes drying racks, collapsible crates to underbed storage containers, mirrors to laundry bags, this handy helper has it all.

Send: LSASE
Ask For: Dorm Essentials Checklist
Mail To: The Complete Collegiate
490 Rte. 46 East
Fairfield, NJ 07704

HUNGRY KITTY
Cat Pin

This charming **cat pin** makes the purr-fect accessory to any outfit. Made of resin by artisan Eddie Walker, the pin features an adorable striped cat munching on a bright red watermelon. This hungry feline is a welcome addition to any jewelry box.

Send: $2.00 P&H
Ask For: Eddie Walker Cat Pin
Mail To: Kaye's Holiday—Dept. CP
6N021 Meredith Rd.
Maple Park, IL 60151

PERSONALIZED PAGING
Code Card

Now you can send pager messages that contain more than just a callback number. With this **FREE code card,** you use numeric codes to indicate your special message. Tell someone you love them or ask if they want to meet later for a bite to eat. Motorola has developed a list of clever codes to make paging more personal.

Send: Your name & address
Ask For: Pager Code Card
Mail To: Motorola
c/o Geltzer & Co., Inc.
1301 Sixth Ave., 14th Floor
New York, NY 10019

PLEASE, MR. POSTMAN
Personalized Picture Postcards

Turn those 35mm photos from your latest vacation or special occasion into **personalized picture postcards** to send to family and friends. Available in packs of 12 in either 3½" x 5" or 4" x 6" sizes, these cards meet all postal requirements. Simply peel off the cover paper to expose the permanent adhesive, attach your photo, and write the address and personal message in the space provided. The card also has a pop-out easel for horizontal or vertical display. Great for birth announcements, invitations, holiday greetings, and more.

Send: $2.00 P&H for 12; $3.75 for 24 (please specify size)
Ask For: Personalized Picture Postcards
Mail To: Picture Postcards
P.O. Box 131
Buffalo, NY 14223-0131

Index

audio cassettes, 19

basketry, 45
beauty aids, 76, 79
bookmarks, 17, 20, 34
books
    activity, 32
    comic, 6
    game, 25
    shape, 26
    storybooks, 18
    writing for children's, 92
bow maker, 42

car care, 98, 99, 100, 101, 103
cards
    flash cards, 14
    note cards, 73
    postcards, 16, 126
certificates, 7
classroom, freebies for, 6–15, 78, 85, 86, 91, 93, 94, 107
clay, modeling, 53. See also dough
consumer education, 15, 87, 89, 92, 93, 105, 108
crafts, 40–53, 56

debt management, 95, 107
dolls, 16, 46, 53, 74
dough, play, 9, 48. See also clay

erasers, 16, 20

fashions, 69
fingerprinting, 9
foam art, 29, 47, 49
food and beverages, 54–63, 89. See also recipes
football fan packages, 113
FREEBIES Magazine offer, 5, 128

games, 23, 25, 30
gifted and talented, students, 7
gift ideas, 36, 47, 70, 72
greenhouse kit, 66

health, 76–79, 80, 81, 86
history
    American heroes, 13

Civil War map, 15
Constitution facts, 11
Federal Reserve System, 6
home, freebies for, 64–75
hostel information, 102, 103
hotel directory, budget, 104

Internet Web sites, 107–111
investments, 96, 108, 109

jewelry, 17, 31, 36, 80, 82, 125

kite making, 49

lesson plans, 8, 15, 94, 107
loans, for students, 90, 95

magazines, 5, 94, 128. See also newsletters; publications
magic tricks, 21, 27
math aids, 10, 14, 87
modeling clay, 53. See also dough

Native American crafts, 43, 52
newsletters, 59, 78, 83, 86, 92, 95, 102, 124
note cards, 73

ordering information, 4–5
ornaments, holiday, 28, 36, 43, 48, 52

painting activities, 45, 50
parenting, 70, 80, 88, 97
pencils, 39
pencil toppers, 26
pen pals, 6
pets and animals, freebies for, 83–85
playing cards, 38
postcards, 16, 126
posters, 12, 13, 71
potpourri, 42, 51
publications, 70, 85, 87, 90, 91, 112
puzzles, 24

recipes. See also food and beverages
    chicken, 61
    dough, 9

eggs, 62
French's Onions, 55
grilling, 57
legumes, 60
lemon, 56, 63
oatmeal, 59
pears, 62
popcorn, 54, 56
quick gourmet meals, 57
rice dishes, 61
recycling, 11
retirement planning, 96, 109
ribbons, 12
rubber stamps, 8, 10, 18, 31

sachets, 42, 51
safety guides
    automobile, 98, 99, 100, 104
    crib, 65
    eye, 82
    fire, 73
    Internet, 106
    skating, 113
    toy, 72
    travel, 101
school supplies, 14, 27, 41
science ideas magazine, 94
scrapbooks, 50
seed packets, 8, 63, 64, 66, 67, 68
sewing, 40, 48, 51, 124
Social Security benefits, 91, 108
software, educational, 86
sports
    fan packages, 113–114
    Internet access, 111
    team addresses, 115–123
stencils, 34, 37, 45
stickers, 10, 19, 21, 22, 23, 24, 29, 32, 33, 35, 37, 39
student education loans, 90, 95

travel and tourism, 98–105, 110

wing badges, 28
World Wide Web sites, 107–111

yo-yo tricks, 22, 95

FREE FREE FREE

Something for nothing!!! There are hundreds of dollars worth of useful, informative, and fun items in each issue of *FREEBIES* Magazine. Each issue, published five times a year (for over 22 years), features at least 100 **FREE** and almost-free offers. You'll get household information, catalogs, recipes, health advice, kids' toys, jewelry, and more. Every offer of every issue is yours for **FREE**, or for a small postage-and-handling charge!

Have you purchased a "Free Things" book before—only to find that the items were unavailable? That won't happen with FREEBIES—all of our offers are authenticated (and verified for accuracy) with the suppliers!

❒ **YES!** Send me 5 issues for only $7.95.

❒ **YES!** I want to save even more. Send me 10 issues for only $9.95.

❒ Payment Enclosed, or Charge my ❒ VISA ❒ MasterCard

Card Number _ _ _ _ _ _ _ _ _ _ _ _ _ _ _ _   Exp. Date _____

Name_____

Address_____

City_____ State _____ Zip_____

Cardholder's Signature_____

Daytime Phone #
( ) _____
(in case we have a question about your subscription)

Send to: *FREEBIES Magazine*/Teacher Offer
1135 Eugenia Place, Carpinteria, CA 93014-5025